Master
Meditations

Master Meditations

a
SPIRITUAL
DAYBOOK

By **Dr. Donald Curtis**

IBS Press, Inc.
Santa Monica, California

IBS PRESS, INC.
744 Pier Avenue
Santa Monica, CA 90405
(213) 450-6485

IBS PRESS FIRST PRINTING, JULY 1990

ISBN 1-877880-03-5

Manufactured in the United States of America

Dedication

To all who seek the Kingdom within. . .

All things proceed from the Quiet Mind.
—ANCIENT CHINESE AXIOM

Other books by Dr. Donald Curtis

Your Thoughts Can Change Your Life
How to Be Great
The Christ-Based Teachings
The Way of the Christ
Finding the Christ
Science of Mind in Daily Living
Human Problems and How to Solve Them
You Are a Wonderful Person
Live It Up
Daily Power for Joyful Living
40 Steps to Self-Mastery
Cosmic Awareness
Master Meditations
Songs of the Soul
Ten Steps to Personal Power
The Christ Way Lessons
New Age Understanding
How to Be Happy and Successful
How to Be a Wonderful Person
Love and Marriage
Twenty-Third Psalm

Contents

How to Use This Book

"My purpose is to become as nearly perfect as I can, to discover the Spirit in myself and in others, to meet my responsibilities, to increase my powers and to move forward in pursuing my goals."

Master Meditations: A Spiritual Daybook is designed to be used by you, not just as a reader but as the writer of your own spiritual unfoldment. This unique and powerful book will enable you to chronicle your progress on your life path.

Read the meditation for the month and, then, the daily meditation each time you pick up this book. Read the joyful, inspiring meditations aloud and silently. Memorize them. Ponder on them as you go about your daily activities. During the day or at the end of the day, whichever is most convenient for you, write down your thoughts. For example, after a meditation on joy, I wrote, "I found joy in every encounter today. I am learning that when I am happy and peaceful inside, everyone responds to my inner joy."

After a meditation on prosperity, you may have insights about any limitations that are keeping you from a full and abundant life. Or you may write down creative ideas for increasing your prosperity, or chart your

"Deep and abiding faith dissolves all fear. My fear dissolves as soon as I reveal and examine it. What am I afraid of? Nothing! 'Fear knocked at the door. Faith answered. No one was there.'"

progress in life not by how many dollars you have amassed, but by the quality of good use to which you put your life and the ways in which you benefit the world.

For the section on faith, you might take a look at what you really believe. Whatever your personal way of worship or whatever particular religious belief you subscribe to, examine the ways in which you live your faith. What does your life say about what you believe?

By asking yourself searching questions and writing down your insights, you may use this journal as a tool for life-affirming change. You will be able to see yourself and your relation to the world with new eyes of perception.

Perhaps you have goals you have not yet reached. Perhaps there are behavior patterns you sincerely want to change. Perhaps you simply want to express more love, more wholeness, more joy. Perhaps you have a dream that you want to come true. Perhaps you want mastery in your life.

Be prepared! At the end of the year, you will be a far different person than when you began this journey. As each master meditation becomes a part of you, your spiritual life will deepen and your dreams will come true.

*"Today, I learn the
lessons of the soul. I am
embarked upon the most
beautiful journey of
unfoldment. I approach
the lessons of the soul
with a desire to change,
a desire to grow, a desire
to experience."*

Master Meditations can be started at any time in the year. Although there are meditations for each day and each month of the year, the point at which you start your master meditations is up to you. Each year offers new possibilities for joyful mastery.

You may want to keep *Master Meditations* by your bedside or at your desk. Although it is a private chronicle, it can also be used in prayer groups as a meditation adjunct and a self-help, spiritual learning tool.

Congratulations! You have just made a commitment to mastering your life. A joyful journey awaits you!

—BettyClare Moffatt, M.A.
    Editor and Publisher,
    Master Meditations: A Spiritual Daybook
    Author, *Gifts for the Living*

Master
Meditations

January

▪ L I F E ▪

I AM THANKFUL FOR NEW LIFE

Today, **I am filled with new life.** I am resurrected. I am healed. I am enthusiastic. I am alive, alert and awake. I go forward into this day filled with joy and enthusiasm.

I ask myself some questions: "Do I have a positive philosophy?", "Do I have a philosophy fit to live by?", "Do I have a self fit to live with?", "Do I have a world fit to live in?"

When I ask myself if I have a world fit to live in, I remember the angel who was complaining about the state of the universe and all the things that were wrong. God said, "If you don't like it the way it is, why don't you go and make a better one?"

That is what I am going to do today. I am going out to make a better world. I am going to start with myself. The thousand mile journey begins by taking the first step.

Today is the first day of the rest of my life. 1
Today is the best day I have ever known. I make
the most of this day. I make the most of myself
and I help other people to make the most of
themselves.

My purpose is to become as nearly perfect
as I can, to discover the Spirit in myself and in
others, to meet my responsibilities, to increase
my powers and to move forward in pursuing my
goals.

As I learn more and become more—I can do
and give more. This is a wonderful day in which
to realize my full potential.

I am on top of the world today. I give thanks for 2
the privilege of living and living well. I feel the
surge of life moving through me and I am filled
with the Living Presence of the Spirit. God is
Life. I am a living expression of God's Reality.

The way is unfolding before me. Truth is
being expressed through me. Life is what I live. I
am full of energy and power.

3 *My body is filled with vitality and my mind is filled with vitality.* I am attuned to creative, abundant life on every level. Life is in free, full flow through me today. I am filled with life. Life everywhere. Life in the world. Life in the heavens. Life in nature. Life in all people. Life in all living things. Life in me.

I dedicate my life to all that is noble, fine and good. I dedicate my life to doing God's Work. My life is God's Life, expressing Itself in every part of my experience.

4 *I give thanks for life and the privilege of living it.* I give thanks for the spiritual energy that surges through my entire being, making me whole, and giving me focus and purpose. I enjoy living life!

This is a beautiful and wonderful day to live—a wonderful opportunity to grow. I give thanks for the success in my life. I give thanks for the prosperity which touches every part of my life.

I feel the flow of life replenishing me. I am alive and experiencing the abundance of the universe.

I have life in my body. I have purpose in my activities. I am a continuous expression of God in action.

I focus on all bright, beautiful and good things and they become a part of everything I do. I give thanks for this bright and beautiful day. I am thankful for the wonderful experience of life.

All that I seek in life unfolds in ways more beautiful than I could have dreamed.

5

I am poised and centered in consciousness and nothing can disturb the calm serenity of my soul. The pulsating action of pure, abundant life moves through my being, healing me and uplifting me.

Life is a wonderful experience. As I go forth into this beautiful day, I am filled with the adventure of living. I am filled with purpose, dedication, devotion, discipline.

6

7 *Life is in free, full flow through me today.* I am enriched in my consciousness of spiritual oneness. God is all of me. I am that part of God which I can understand.

I am made in the image and likeness of God, and I strive to be perfect even as God is Perfect. I experience perfection in all parts of my life, my work and my personal relationships.

8 *All is unfolding in the consciousness of rich, full living.* God is in charge of my life.

I am living life eternal and transcendant today. There are more years in my life and more life in my years. There is life in my mind and I am alert. There is life in my heart and I am loved. There is life in my body and I am strong.

....
....
....
....
....
....
....
....
....
....
....

9 *I feel the vital love of the Universal Spirit giving me new life, health, fullness and abundance on every level.*

I am a whole person and I am attuned. Where any problem or challenge seems to be, God is there first. I am always aware of my spiritual nature. I am a spiritual being.

....
....
....
....
....
....
....
....
....
....
....
....

10 *I experience God's Life moving through every level of my being.* Life is good. Life is wonderful. I give thanks for this life which has been given to me to participate in.

I am thankful for love to express and to receive. I am thankful for joy to feel in my heart and to express each moment of this day. I realize now what a great and wonderful adventure life is.

11 ***Today, I experience my inner life.*** Today, I am aware of the richness of life. Thank You, God, for this life which has been given to me to live and for love which has been given to me to express.

Thank You for oneness. Thank You for wholeness. Thank You for the Living Light of the Spirit that moves through me, today, enlivening me and making me whole.

I feel vitality in my mind, my heart, my body and my soul. I feel complete on every level.

12 ***Thank You, God, for this day of Eternity.*** I feel the abundant flow of life. I am conscious of love and generosity everywhere.

Life is in free, full, flow through me. I am attuned to all that is bright, beautiful and good. God's Healing Presence circulates through my mind, heart, soul and body, making me whole on every level.

....
....
....
....
....
....
....
....
....
....
....
....

As I move closer to the realization of my true and perfect self, I have a strong sense that all is well. God is in His Heaven and all is right with the world. I am strong, I am vital, I am happy, I am successful, I am free.

13

This bright, beautiful day is mine to live. I live it fully. I am in tune with the Infinite. I feel pure energy pulsating in every part of my being. I am lifted to a greater awareness than I have ever known.

....
....
....
....
....
....
....
....
....
....
....
....

I view life from a higher point of awareness. I am involved in it, but I can be objective and remove myself from trivial concerns. I transform all negative energies into vital and perfect life.

14

Quietly now, I attune myself to the Infinite Healing Presence. I have an overwhelming feeling of oneness and of power.

Today, I am part of the mainstream of life. The Law of Right Action is working in my life. I am in tune with Perfection.

15 *All difficult situations resolve themselves in my life as I let God guide me.* I have the confidence I need to be a successful, happy person.

Today, I dedicate myself to being the best that I can be. I dedicate myself to doing the best job that I can do. I dedicate myself to helping other people whenever and wherever I can.

I dedicate myself to taking care of my body, my heart and my mind first so that I can live to my fullest potential.

16 *I give thanks for this bright, beautiful day.* I give thanks for the fullness of life. I give thanks for the gifts of love, of joy, of wisdom, of beauty, of creativity.

In the blessed quiet of my meditation, I discover the Presence of Divine Spirit. I discover abundant life springing up into full and perfect expression within me.

I am attuned spiritually, emotionally, mentally and physically, to pure Light.

....

....

....

....

....

....

....

....

....

....

....

17

I am successful in every part of my life. I do my best to express my highest potential at all times.

I give thanks for the privilege of living God's Life today. Life is a tremendous opportunity to express the Spirit of God in my world. I am a channel through which God may flow forth into outer manifestation of good.

I experience the glorious adventure of life fully today.

....

....

....

....

....

....

....

....

....

....

....

18

I see life as an opportunity to share with others the great insights of the Kingdom, the great reality of the inner world, the great harmony which comes from a deep understanding of God.

This is a day to live. Life is to be cherished.

I take full advantage of living today. Life is in free, full, flow through me and I relish each moment of it. I give thanks for God's Life, expressing itself through me. I give thanks for the realization of my full and perfect expression.

19 *Throughout my life, I seek to transcend the difficulties and worries of the external world.* I seek first the Kingdom and all other things are added unto me. God's Blessings are manifesting in my life as abundant health, happiness, success, freedom and love.

I am joyfully attuned to the Infinite Source of life. The Spirit within is beckoning me to join in praise and blessing.

20 *There is One Life.* This life is God. This life is whole. This life is perfect. This life is my life now.

I aspire, today, to be vital and alert all the days of my life. I aspire to have more years in my life and more life in my years.

Life is the Spirit moving through me. Life is Light. Life is God in action.

....
....
....
....
....
....
....
....
....
....
....

My mind is marvelous. Every time I think, I set creativity into motion in my life. God's Mind is my mind now. God's Mind is thinking, feeling, believing, understanding and acting through my mind.

Life is the Spirit in action through my being. It is uplifting me, sustaining me and manifesting in every part of my world.

21

....
....
....
....
....
....
....
....
....
....
....

I dedicate myself and my life to God today. This is my day of infinite possibilities. This is a wonderful day to make my own, to do the wonderful things I want to do, to be the wonderful things I want to be.

This is a day of sheer joy, a day of unfolding spiritual expression, a day of Light. I focus my attention upon the lessons of the soul, upon attainment of: peace, love, understanding, gentleness and purity.

22

23 *I give thanks for this day of beauty.* I give thanks for the privilege of living, learning, loving and growing. I give thanks for the opportunity to pray, to meditate, to study, to contemplate the great Inner Reality of the Spirit. I give thanks for the chance to be that which God knows me to be—a full and perfect expression of Himself.

Today, I feel the richness of the Spirit within me. I feel abundant good flowing through my whole being and I am lifted to a higher awareness of the beauty and the wisdom of life.

24 *In the blessed quiet, I contemplate nature, life, and my beingness.* This is a day of vital importance. What a gift a day is! A new one is presented to us every twenty-four hours. Every ending is a new beginning.

Right this instant, I start a new chain of creative action through my thoughts and my feelings. Everything I do has an effect in the world.

I am in tune with the Infinite. I move in consciousness of love, peace and harmony.

My state of awareness is my true prosperity. I am rich in love, in peace, in faith. I am expressing prosperity in my life now and always.

Infinite Life is unfolding within me. This is a beautiful day to live, a beautiful day to sing, a beautiful day to love, a beautiful day to grow, a beautiful day to worship. I go forward into this day filled with vitality.

This is the first day of the rest of my life. This is the best day I have ever known. Today, I listen to God.

25

I give thanks for health, for inspiration, for joy and for the Light that guides me through life. I go forward enthusiastically to live the life that God has given me. I may not know what is ahead for me, today, but I know it can only be good. I go forward with the anticipation of the perfect unfoldment of all impending events.

Only good can grace my day. Only good can take place in my mind, my heart, my soul, my body and my world. Divine Order and Right Action are present in everything that I am and in everything that I do.

26

27 ***Thank You, God, for this day and the privilege of living it.*** I know only good today. I give thanks for air to breathe, for water to drink, for food to eat. I give thanks for the opportunities and privileges that come to me during this glorious, wonderful experience of life.

I give thanks for other people. I learn to understand them. I learn to share with them. I learn from them, and, by letting love flow forth from me, I am able to benefit them and myself.

28 ***Thank You, God, for the great opportunities that have come into my life.*** I laugh loud and long today. I love life and I love to live. Bubbling up from within me is a well of everlasting joy, energy and all good things.

I look out upon my world, today, and I find that it is good—very good indeed. I give thanks for life and for the privilege of living it. I give thanks for the opportunity to express, to know, to do and to be.

Thank You, God, for the privilege of living. 29
Thank You for the opportunity of expanding my
understanding. Thank You for this glorious life.
This is a bright and beautiful day to experience
the fullness of life.

I bubble over with enthusiasm because life
is a great and marvelous adventure. Life is the
greatest gift from God.

Today, I am a complete expression of physical, 30
emotional, mental and spiritual health. I am in
tune with God. God is the Source of my supply.
God is my very life.

I know that there is nothing that God and I
together cannot handle. I wholeheartedly greet
everything that comes my way: new challenges,
new opportunities, new gains.

31 ***God's Abundance is everywhere apparent in my world.*** I am in tune with life and life is in tune with me. I am one with the forces of nature. I am part of the spiritual harmony of the universe.

My success in life depends upon my prevailing mental and emotional attitude. I always see the glass as half full rather than half empty. Even though there may be problems, challenges and vicissitudes, I know that they are all for my ultimate good.

I try to learn from my mistakes. I gain strength from challenging experiences and I move forward in my growth.

I am in my right place, doing my right work. All things are unfolding in perfect order. Divine Wisdom guides me in everything that I do and in everything that I am.

⸳⸳⸳⸳⸳⸳⸳⸳⸳⸳⸳⸳⸳⸳ Monthly Goals ⸳⸳⸳⸳⸳⸳⸳⸳⸳⸳⸳⸳⸳⸳

_____

_____

_____

_____

_____

_____

_____

_____

_____

_____

_____

_____

_____

_____

_____

_____

_____

▪ L O V E ▪

GOD IS LOVE

Love is the greatest force uniting the world. Love is the language of the soul. Love is the great affirmation. Love is that inner feeling of union and oneness. Love is the desire to unite with the object of our affection and our attention.

Today, I meditate upon love. Love is God. Love is the fulfilling of the Law. Love heals me, blesses me, uplifts me and gives me life.

I am filled with Divine Love. I am filled with Divine Light. I am filled with Divine Joy. I am filled with the Presence and the Power of God flowing through me as love.

I love life and I love to live. I love to do the work which God has given me to do and be a part of this wonderful world. I love all that is noble, fine, beautiful and good. I love God. I love other people. I love myself.

Thank You, God, for love. I am filled with love. I am filled with kindness. I am compassionate and altruistic.

My heart, my mind, my soul and my body are blessed by Divine Love. God's Love for His Creation is expressed through me in every vibration of my thought and feeling, in every cell of my body.

I love because He first loved us. I am capable of pure, strong, wholesome feeling. I am a loving person. I am filled with "agape." Spiritual love is permanently conditioned into my consciousness.

1

I am a loving person. I am free from anything unlike the Nature of God.

I am in love with life. I am in love with God. I am in love with peace.

I let my love come out into expression. I think about love. I feel love. Love permeates my entire being.

I feel a deep and tender love for all people everywhere. I feel love toward the whole universe. Through the eyes of love, I see all people as God's children. I love and bless my family, my friends, my fellow workers, my neighbors.

2

3 *God is expressed in my life as the love that I feel for all things.* The great, healing power of love flows through me and enriches me. Love is the greatest power in the world.

I forgive myself for all past, real or fancied wrongs. If anyone has done wrong to me, I forgive that person. I free myself from fear and guilt.

I move forward with strong and vital love today. I love this day and the privilege of living it. I love other people and the privilege of knowing them. I love myself and the privilege of being a perfect expression of God.

4 *I love my work.* I go forward with joy do those things which are to be done by me. I love God. God loves me. All is well in my world today.

I experience love, today, in my mind, in my heart, in my soul, in every part of my life. Love—the language of the soul—speaks through me. Love makes all things right in my world.

**If I have love, I don't really need anything 5
more.** If I have love, then I have enough to do all
that God has given me to do—to live happily,
harmoniously and healthfully, and to help my fellow human family members.

Love is the new commandment for me. God's
Love is circulating through me. I am a child of
God and a creature of love.

Love is the expression of God's Abundance in
my life. All good is flowing into my life now. I am
truly blessed.

**As I grow and unfold today, I feel God's Love 6
everywhere in my world.** I am filled with love
and all is well. I feel the power of love lifting me
to a higher dimension of life. As I love, all aspects
of my life become harmonious, orderly, happy
and peaceful.

In deep spiritual love, I am attuned to God
within. His Light shines through every expression
of my life.

7 *Thank You, God, for the love that envelops me now.* Love flows forth from me into my world. I love life. I love other people. I love myself. I love my work. I love the past, the present and the future. I love the challenges that come my way because it is through them that I grow. I am completely positive today.

I am a loving person. If there is a problem or difficulty of any kind, I surround it with love and blessing, and it becomes an opportunity for me to express God in my life.

8 *My love is enthusiasm for life.* Joyously, I go forward, loving everything, experiencing inspiration in every aspect of my life.

Love makes all things whole in my life. The love that flows from God lifts me to a higher dimension and to a higher level of expression. Love brings Divine Order and Right Action into my life. Harmony and peace come from God's Love within me.

Thank You, God, for love and the privilege of **9**
loving abundantly. Love makes me whole.

Love is the ultimate prosperity. As I pray, and feel the Infinite Light flowing through me, I thank God, from Whom all things come.

The consciousness of love is in all that I am and all that I do. The loving Essence of God is apparent in every part of my being. I am in tune with Infinite Love.

I am rich in love today. **10**

Today, I meditate on brotherhood and cooperation. I am a brother. I am a child of God. I am part of the human family. I feel a deep sense of kinship with all mankind. There are billions of people in my family—the human family.

Spiritual love is the love that sees God in everyone.

11 *Today, I behold the Spirit in everyone I meet.* I see love, I see joy, I see all good and wonderful things in everyone. Love unites us all. Love unites me to the great fellowship of humanity.

Each day, I have the opportunity of revealing my Divinity to everyone I touch. I have the privilege of living, learning and growing with others in the great expanse of our universe.

12 *Thank You, God, for fellowship and cooperation among people.* Thank You for this journey which we are upon together. Thank You for the opportunity to help each other and learn from each other.

Love is fellowship with others. This is a beautiful day to live, to love, to learn, to serve.

....

Love lifts me above the negative energy of life today. God loves me, God loves my life, God loves what I am doing, God loves all good things. When I love God, I am rewarded with His Infinite Blessings flowing into my life and the world around me. **13**

Love means forgiveness in every way for me. I am attentive to forgiveness in my life. All guilt is dissolved from my consciousness. I do not condemn myself. I forgive myself. I give up all limited, worn-out, false ideas. I replace them with new ideas, new awareness, new understanding.

....

Having experienced the consequences of past errors, I am now free to go forward into life to do those things which God has given me to do. I bury the dead past. I direct all my energy into constructive, purposeful endeavor. **14**

Today is a day of love. I fast from hostility and resentment. I feast on love. Love is the only power in the world. Love is God.

I love the very thought of experiencing Reality—the peace, the joy and all of the wonderful aspects of being a spiritual being.

15 ***How can I be of value in my life?*** By being a valuable person. By doing valuable things. By loving myself.

I give thanks, today, for the precious pearls that God has given me: love, life, peace, awareness. As these great gifts are given to me, I look for ways to give to others. I look for ways to serve and to do good.

I serve by cleansing my thoughts, by filling my heart with love, by engaging in meaningful activities. I give thanks for the value I can be in helping myself, in helping others, in doing good in my world.

16 ***I am of value in my life.*** Divine Love blesses and increases all that I have, all that I give and all that I receive.

Love is a matter of giving and receiving. I receive abundantly. I give generously. God gives me all good and wonderful things. I return my gratitude, my love and my devotion to Him.

I am grateful for His Love. I am grateful for His Good.

As I attune myself to the Spirit, I feel the Spirit flowing through me and blessing me with love. This is a time of loving realization—loving life, loving God, loving myself, loving all people.

17

Quietly and softly, the Infinite Healing Presence is raying out, cleansing and revitalizing my being. I feel Divine Love surrounding me and making me whole on every level and in every way.

I am attuned to the Infinite Love, the Infinite Light, the Infinite Presence of God. The loving, healing, vitalizing energy of pure Spirit is moving through me now.

18

Love turns on the flow of life. Love makes me whole. I am grateful for God's loving gifts of life, health and prosperity. He is the Source of my supply.

19 *God's Love is manifested through the act of giving and receiving.* God's Love unites all.

Love comes from inner attunement with the Spirit. Love occurs in the Presence of God. I open myself up to God. I am a channel through which the universal energy flows.

I am of great value in my world. I am of value to myself and others. I think good thoughts, I feel good feelings, I say good things and I do good in my world.

20 *I am a co-creator with God.* I create a positive reality in which I express God in all that I am and in all that I do.

I give thanks for the privilege of being of value to God and mankind today. I am crowned with honor and glory. I am an expression of God. I am made in His image and likeness.

God loves me enough to have blessed me with life and love. It is up to me to think well of His Creation and to love myself as He loves me.

Thank You, God, for the wonder, the beauty and the joy of being Your child. I strive to be a loving child of God in all that I am and in all that I do.

21

I give thanks for this day of love, this day of beauty, this day of worship, this day of contemplation of the great Realms of the Spirit. As I contemplate God's Greatness, I feel it flowing into me and manifesting everywhere in my world.

This is a day of bright, beautiful and joyous love.

22

Today, I am determined to keep my mind clear, my heart warm, my body pure, my actions controlled and my words kind. I exist on all of these levels simultaneously. All of my parts are integrated.

My heart is my soul, my inner core. The Spirit within me is vital Love, enlivening my mind, my actions, my world.

23 *I am loving today.* I am whole and sound in my constant contact with the Spirit of God. I am one with the Spirit of Love.

God is all of me. I am that part of God which I can understand. There is only Perfect God, perfect man, perfect being. I surrender my humble self and the Infinite Self takes over.

Love is in free, full flow through me today. I feel a tremendous resurgence of loving energy in my mind, my heart, my soul and my body.

24 *I am a strong and vital expression of love in action.* Love has deep meaning for me. God is always waiting within with His Abundant Love.

In the blessed quiet, the power of love flows into my being. God's Love is in my mind, my heart, my soul, my body and in my world of affairs. I am attuned to all that is bright, beautiful and loving.

I feel the energy of God's Love today. The power of love flows through my being. Love is feeling good about everything and everyone. Love is coming to terms with the hurt and the pain. **25**

I am a loving, prosperous being. I share my prosperity with others through my love. I receive prosperity through the love of others. Love is circulating through my being—flowing in and flowing out, giving and receiving, ebb and flow.

I am in tune with the Universal Goodness. The Love of God is in my heart and all is well. During my time of prayer, I establish a consciousness of love in my world. **26**

I am one with God and, at the same time, I am an individualized expression of Him. I am whole, I am happy, I am loved.

27 *God's Love flows through me and I feel harmonious on every level.* I keep my heart warm and love flowing abundantly in my world. I keep my mind clear, my body pure, my actions controlled and my words kind. I keep myself integrated spiritually, mentally, emotionally and physically.

I attune myself to love. I can handle anything that comes my way. As I go forward, I let love flow forth from me and brighten my world.

28 *Love is flowing into me from above.* I love my neighbor as I love myself. Love is the great unifying force of the universe. I am filled with love today.

Love turns on the flow of life. Love is God and this love—this affinity for good—makes all life whole.

I love life. I love health. I love all of the gifts that God has given to me.

God's Love is vitalized through giving and receiving. God's Love is expressed in me now. Today, I have warm feelings toward all beings. I love God. I love others. I love myself. I love life. I love my work.

I love this great, big bright wonderful world. I love the sun that shines, the stars that twinkle, the moon that glows, and the bright, blue sky overhead. This beautiful day is evidence of God's Love for me. I rejoice in it.

I am grateful for God's Love. I am grateful for the love that I feel inside myself. I love Truth. I love myself. I love all people. I love the great human family. I love my country.

29

Monthly Goals

March

▪ D I V I N E   O R D E R ▪

DIVINE ORDER IS ESTABLISHED

Divine Order and Right Action are operating in everything that I am and in everything that I do.

I may not know what is ahead for me, today, but I know that it can only be good. I go forward into this day with confidence and enthusiasm. I anticipate all impending events with expectation of good. Only good can grace my day. Only good can take place in my mind, in my heart, in my soul, in my body and in my world of affairs. Divine Order is established.

I am on top of things today. I see this day as an opportunity to learn and to grow. I am prosperous as a result of my positive attitude toward life, toward people, toward everything I see around me. If all is not as it should be, then I try to help bring about positive change. When I have done what I can, I let Divine Order take its course.

I am grateful for God's Universe and the privilege of living in it. Everything has a place and meaning in the world and I am grateful for this, too. Divine Order and Right Action prevail in my world today.

I establish discipline in all of my daily activities. I am in charge of myself and my actions. He who conquers the city is great; he who conquers himself is mighty.

I make up my mind to do my best at all times. When confronted with a choice, I choose that which is good, that which God would choose.

1

I grow, I learn, I expand. I am on the upward way. I affirm perfect order in all of my experiences. I know that only good can come my way.

I absorb the goodness in life. Good energy is moving into me, taking residence in my being on every level. God in action through me produces my health, my prosperity, my freedom and my happiness.

Today is a great opportunity to express God in all that I do. I attune myself to the Living Spirit and a world of possibilities is opened up to me.

2

3 *Thank You, God, for making me and all of my fellow human beings in Your likeness.* I strive to live up to Your example. I strive for perfection.

Today, I keep before me the ideal of perfect order in my life. I do all that I can to follow the inner guidance of the Spirit, to be all that God knows me to be—a complete expression of Himself.

There is One Perfect Reality, One Perfect Truth.

4 *I am attuned to order and harmony, and, from this center of awareness, I go through my day.* I set meaningful goals for today. This is a beautiful day to learn and to grow. I know that life has meaning and purpose, and I do those things which further my goals.

I set inner goals of growth: to be more loving, to have a greater understanding of God. I then set outer goals of achievement in my life. I move forward in this manner.

Thank You, God, for the fulfillment of my goals.

_____
_____
_____
_____
_____
_____
_____
_____
_____
_____

Today, I get my priorities in order. First, I clear my mind, I warm my heart and I heal my body. Then, I am ready to go forward into the world with confidence and enthusiasm.

There is One Life. This life is God. This life is whole. This life is perfect. This life is my life now. As I believe this in my inner core, everything comes together perfectly.

5

_____
_____
_____
_____
_____
_____
_____
_____
_____
_____

I am in tune with the Infinite Invisible Power flowing through me and lifting me to a higher level of good. I meditate, today, upon discipline, devotion, dedication.

I take my life in hand and I establish authority over it. I go forward into the world secure in the knowledge that I am the master of my fate.

I know that my thoughts and actions produce a reaction. The state of my consciousness deter-mines what I experience in my world.

6

7 *I give thanks for order and purpose in my life today.* I have a positive mental and emotional attitude. I am confident that the best is going to happen today. I consciously create positive circumstances in which to experience the best in my life.

I have a self fit to live with. I have a philosophy fit to live by. I have a world fit to live in. I give thanks that this is so.

8 *God is with me.* His Rod and His Staff they comfort me. I am uplifted. I fly upward with eagle's wings toward the Secret Place of the Most High.

I am a positive force. Today, as I face the challenges of the work-a-day world, as I begin new projects and put new ideas into expression, I am filled with joy and purpose.

Today, and each day, is the beginning of a new experience. I am filled with the consciousness of the Spirit. I tune in to my Higher Self and good unfolds in every part of my being.

....
....
....
....
....
....
....
....
....
....
....

I am a positive force in my life. I am completely attuned to the expression of God.

I am in control today. Whenever anything difficult comes up in my world, even if it is a bitter struggle or a tough proposition, I say, "Thank You, God, for this evidence of Your love for me," for through this means I grow.

9

....
....
....
....
....
....
....
....
....
....
....

The Spirit that dwells within me does the work and I can handle anything. I master the science of crisis control. I keep calm in every situation and all tension, pressure, anxiety, worry and other negative feelings dissolve.

When I am confronted with a problem of any kind, I think of God instead, and the solution to the problem suddenly becomes crystal clear.

10

11 **Today, I get clearly in mind what it is I want.** I develop a strong conviction that it is already mine and I do everything that I can to bring it about. Then I release it, I give thanks and I let Divine Order prevail.

In my time of quiet, I review those things which are necessary to achieve my goals. I apply myself diligently. I think clearly and keep focused on the goal at hand. I do a good job of living.

12 **I release this prayer to the Spirit above and I give thanks that all good is done already.** I give thanks for this day of living, loving, learning and growing. I give thanks for the experience of God's Wonder. Today, I am on top of things. I am on top of my work and all of my relationships are working well.

Thank You, God, for work to do. Thank You for pleasures to enjoy. Thank You for air to breathe, for water to drink and for the sun to warm me. Thank You, God, for the great blessings in my life.

My attitude of gratitude raises the energy around me. All good things flow into my life and they flow out to others around me. This is a day of opportunity for me. I paint my picture upon the canvas of life. I am attuned to God's Perfection and I know that the picture which I paint is a masterpiece. My picture reflects the beauty of God's Presence.

13

God creates order, harmony, peace, happiness, health, prosperity, freedom and love in my world.

I picture only good today. I move forward in the direction of my ideal. My goals are definite, my aim is straight, my priorities are clear. I affirm accomplishment and success on every level. I accept myself as a prosperous person because I really am.

14

I give thanks for the inner conviction to do that which God has given me to do. Then, I go out and follow the inner direction to accomplish my goals.

15 ***When I have done all I can do, I let go and give thanks.*** There is an Infinite Supply of all good things and I have everything I need.

God is the One Source. I have all of His Riches and Plenty. I am enriched spiritually, mentally, emotionally, physically and materially.

I share my good with others. I give cheer and encouragement. I express enthusiasm. I help in every way I can.

16 ***I am aware of great opportunities all around me.*** I revel in the great glory of life. I live it fully. I live it abundantly. I am enriched by the wonderful gifts that God has given me.

Success comes from an inner state of mind. Accomplishment comes from clear planning of goals and objectives, and persistence in keeping at it. Success does not come by accident. But I have the power I need to make it happen in my life.

I achieve success by doing those things which are the mark of a successful person. I am successful within and I express it in my world.

I am free from old, negative patterns of thinking and behaving. I am free from failure. I forgive myself and others for all error and all hurt.

If there is any individual who has done me wrong, I surround him with Light. I free him by saying, "In the center of the Light, you stand. I release you and let you go on your way. I give you freedom, and, thereby, I claim my own."

17

Today, I am freed from all limitations. I reject old, negative conditioning as I move forward into a bright, new life. I am free in faith, free in love and free in forgiveness.

Good is within me, therefore, all good things take place in my world. I experience bright, beautiful happiness in my life. I look forward to all impending events with enthusiasm and expectation of good.

I am freed from my small, petty self as I move into a higher level of consciousness and I become one with God.

18

19 *I have the power of choice.* I know that whatever I choose comes into expression in my life.

Today, I choose all that is good. I choose to make contact with God. I choose to dwell in the Kingdom within. I choose to find spiritual understanding. I choose to be a better person.

I choose to be an example that others may follow. I choose order, harmony and peace in my world. I choose to be one with God.

20 *I follow the pathway of spirituality from this moment, on to the end of each day.* I am attuned to inner order and purpose, and I live from this reality.

I give thanks for the abundance which is mine today. I give thanks for work to do and for the people who enrich my life. I give thanks for the beautiful lessons of the soul.

Today, I put myself in the driver's seat. I control my thoughts, my feelings and my actions. I keep myself aligned with God. 21

There is but One, and I am one with the One. God is my strength. God is my life. God is my inspiration. God is my love, my faith, my joy, my very being.

When I am confronted with trouble of any kind, I look to God for inspiration to resolve it. I move forward into life filled with the confidence to meet all of life's challenges.

Only good can come into my life because there is only good in my heart, mind and soul. I anticipate all impending events with enthusiasm and expectation of good. 22

Today, I build my spiritual progress out of positive and constructive thoughts, feelings and actions. I affirm that I am a healthy person, whole in every way. I affirm that I am adjusted and focused. I affirm Right Action unfolding in every aspect of my life.

23 *Divine Order is unfolding everywhere in my world.* God has given me the opportunity to make the most of myself and I am grateful.

I put everything in order, today, and bring harmony into my life. My mind and my heart are working together. I am integrated.

In forming within me a bright and beautiful reality, I am ready to go forward to do that which God has given me to do. I contribute to my world. I give to people. I apply my creative efforts toward the betterment of all.

24 *Today, I focus my mind.* I warm my heart. I strengthen my body. I attune my soul.

There is an Eternal Rightness in the universe and I am in tune with it. I focus my consciousness on the One Presence and the One Power in the universe.

....

....

....

....

....

....

....

....

....

....

I release myself from all cares, worries, tensions and anxieties, and I go forward into this day filled with the confidence that everything will unfold in Divine Order. A mind expanded to the dimensions of a greater idea can never return to its original size. God is all of me. I am that part of God which I can understand. **25**

My understanding is growing and unfolding. The more I meditate on my inner life, the more I feel one with the Infinite.

....

....

....

....

....

....

....

....

....

....

....

My mind is bright, alert and in order. I am focused as I go forward into this day. I keep my goals clearly in mind. **26**

I expect the best from myself and I expect the best from other people. I expect to be happy. I expect to be successful. I expect to be healthy. I expect the best to happen all of the time.

27 *I allow others to be free to express themselves the way they choose, just as I claim this freedom myself.* I let things unfold in Divine Order as God intends.

A great abundance of all good things flows from the Kingdom within me. I am attuned to the Greatness of God. I develop a strong conviction that all good is taking place in my life, and it is.

28 *I am here for a definite reason.* I am here to live my life to its fullest potential and to be a complete expression of God.

Everyday, I accomplish mighty things: I express God's Wonder and Glory in all of my actions, I work from the center of Divine Inspiration, I attune myself to the good around me everywhere and I share this good with others.

Thank You, God, for the opportunity to carry out Your Will. Thank You for Divine Order and Right Action in the world.

I use my creative imagination. In the quietness, I see myself as God sees me—His perfect image and likeness. 29

As my imagination takes hold of this idea, I believe that I am a perfect child of God. I form the image of God in my mind—balanced, whole, perfect—and I make it my own.

I feel the tide of rising consciousness moving me to greater understanding, lifting me to greater inspiration. 30

I find true fulfillment, today, as I get in touch with the creativity of life. I am grateful for the privilege of learning, knowing, expressing, sharing. I am grateful for the opportunity to express God in my life. Thank You, God, for helping me to do my very best and inspiring me to new heights of expression.

31

Today, I keep my words kind, my actions controlled, my heart warm, my body pure and my thoughts clear. I move steadily forward. I release negative, petty thoughts and I turn my attention toward the goal at hand.

It doesn't matter what has ruffled my feelings or upset my equilibrium in the past, today I am poised and centered and nothing can disturb the serenity of my soul.

I move steadily forward with my hand in God's Hand. His Arms are around me and I know they will never be taken away. I feel this in my deepest core, my very bloodstream, in the tissues and cells of my body. I am secure in this knowledge.

Monthly Goals

April

▪ P R O S P E R I T Y ▪

THERE IS ABUNDANCE ON EVERY LEVEL

P*rosperity is a state of mind.* I build my prosperity through positive thoughts, feelings, vision. I build my prosperity through discipline, dedication and devotion.

I am a prosperous person on every level. I am spiritually prosperous because I am one with God. All of His Riches and Blessings are mine.

My mind is prosperous because I think only good, positive, constructive thoughts. I am focused and clear about what I want and what I believe.

I am emotionally prosperous because I am a kind, loving, warm person. I share my feelings with others and let them share theirs with me.

I am physically prosperous because I am healthy, strong and whole. I take good care of myself.

I am spiritually prosperous, I am mentally prosperous, I am emotionally prosperous, I am physically prosperous. I experience abundance in every way. I affirm my prosperity every day.

....
....
....
....
....
....
....
....
....
....
....
....

This is my time of prosperity. God is all Wealth. God is my wealth. The mind that is filled with God is filled with abundance. I experience abundance in every part of my life.

1

I attune myself to the abundant life today. The free, full, flow of life is surging through me. I am one with Infinite Abundance.

I give thanks for my prosperity today.

....
....
....
....
....
....
....
....
....
....

God's Abundance is my abundance. The abundant life is my life. I am living it today. I am expressing it. God's Riches are flowing into my life on every level. I experience the wealth of the Kingdom.

2

I accept this good flowing into my life and I give thanks. Thank You, God, for life to live. Thank You for air to breathe. Thank You for water to drink. Thank You for food to eat. Thank You for loving and understanding friends. Thank You for work to do. Thank You for the privilege of learning, loving, sharing and growing.

3 *As my consciousness expands, more good flows into me from the Infinite Source.* I know that God wants me to be successful. God wants me to be healthy, happy and whole. God wants me to realize my full potential. My prosperity is up to me.

My thoughts are cheerful, positive and constructive. I behold the good in everyone. I see the good in every situation. I keep a rich consciousness. I praise God for the blessings which He has given me and the whole human race.

4 *The more I am spiritually aware, the more I find myself in the mainstream of abundance and success.* This is my time of success, health, harmony and all good things.

I am a vital, strong person. What a privilege it is to be alive! I sing out with the joy of living. I love life and I love to live.

My consciousness is whole. I am in tune with the Infinite. I know true prosperity now. Prosperity is answered prayer.

I seek first the Kingdom and all good things are added unto me. All worthwhile things are coming to me. I have an attitude of expectancy.

I am filled with fertile, constructive ideas. I think well about myself. I think well about other people. I think well about my world, about my job and about all parts of my life. I am grateful because I know that good is unfolding through me on every level.

I am successful and prosperous in every way. I carry myself as a prosperous person. Success depends upon my attitude toward a goal. It comes from within.

I am successful when I know that I am successful. I am prosperous when I accept the concept of prosperity in every aspect of my life.

7 *Today, I accept my prosperity.*
I am mentally prosperous because I think positively and creatively. I am emotionally prosperous because I am filled with love. I am physically prosperous because I am strong and whole. I am spiritually prosperous because I am part of God.

8 *I have more than enough to meet all my requirements today.* I experience true prosperity. I am filled with cheer and good will.

I am filled with the riches of the Kingdom. I am filled with all that is wonderful, beautiful and good. The consciousness of Light is within me.

I am filled with vitality which is the true prosperity of my life. All good is flowing into me from above. All good is flowing from me out into my world.

The Spark of Divinity within me is fanned into full flame. I am one with God's great and beautiful universe today.

    The Infinite Abundance is pouring into my life. I am complete and integrated. God's Riches are my riches now.

    All limiting, negative thoughts are dissolved from my mind and replaced by thoughts of all that is bright, beautiful and good.

9

In the Presence of God, I feel myself one with all experience. This is my greatest wealth.

    I am building with the Master Mind. I build my life today. I build temples within my soul. I build my spiritual path.

    I am blessed with God's Abundant Gifts. My heart is filled with love. My mind is filled with Truth. My soul is filled with peace.

10

11 ***Prosperity is built into my life.*** This day and every day is one of prosperity and success. Success is present in every aspect of my life— spiritually, mentally, emotionally, physically and materially.

Prosperity means answered prayer and my prayer is always answered. God is the Source of my supply. All good is in my heart. All good is in my life.

12 ***I am prosperous, today, because I have an attitude of self-worth, love, faith, strength, power.*** My attitude shapes my reality.

My prosperity starts inside. If I have a choice, I always choose the positive, optimistic one. I believe in myself and my prosperity. God is the Source of my supply.

The Law of Abundance flows through me. I am a
channel of love through which all good things are
expressed. Abundance and success come about
in my life.

13

    I am a strong, vital, healthy, happy and suc-
cessful person now. I am rich in the great gifts
that God has given me. I am rich in the bright,
shining, warm sun. The earth is a great and fertile
garden in which to cultivate the abundance that
God has given me.

My prosperity comes from my love for life. Life
is connecting me to everything bright, wonderful
and good.

14

    I have an attitude of dedication and commit-
ment toward life, toward myself, toward my work
and toward other people. I am cheerful in manner. I am purposeful in endeavor. I go forth with
confidence to do those things that are to be done
by me.

15 *I express prosperity in all that I am and in all that I do.* I am a prosperous person. I have an abundance of joy for living. I have an abundance of creative ideas. I have great dedication, devotion and discipline.

I determine the prosperity and success in my world.

16 *I am successful, happy and secure.* God is my prosperity. I give thanks that this is so. I increase my inner prosperity today.

In the blessed quiet, I feel the Presence of God on every level. Thank You, God, for the abundance which is mine. Thank You for the free, full, flow of life which surges through me. Thank You for the awareness of the beauty and the richness of the universe.

I give thanks for the building blocks to construct my life. I am indebted to the One. The riches of the Kingdom are mine today.

I give thanks for the One Source from which all things flow. I give thanks for all good taking place in my life now and always. The energy of the Spirit moves through me, enriching me, enlivening me, uplifting me, making me whole on every level.

17

My mind is clear and my heart is warm. My actions are controlled and purposeful.

Abundance flows through me meeting all of my needs today. I live this day fully and abundantly. I am filled with all good.

As I go about my daily tasks today, I do all as unto the Lord and not unto man. I am the channel through which God expresses His Goodness. I am grateful that this is so.

18

19 *I am living a great, fulfilling life.* I am successful, prosperous and happy. I meet the challenges that confront me with the confidence that the outcome will be successful.

I am rich in the consciousness of abundant life. I am rich in all that God has. I am rich in His Presence everywhere.

My prosperity is my oneness with the One Source. I have more than enough to meet all of my requirements. The love that flows to me and from me, increases and multiplies all good in the universe.

20 *The Law of Abundance is active in my life.* I am the channel through which all good is expressed. I feel my oneness with God completely and abundantly. I am bountiful in Him.

I know that God's Prosperity is ever with me no matter what happens in my outer world. I am free from limitation on every level. My mind is free. My heart is untroubled. Everything is unfolding as it should.

I claim my good. I give thanks for it. I praise the creative power within me through which I am successful. **21**

All parts of my being are integrated and I am blessed with abundant harmony. I am a complete person. All of my energy is focused toward the same goal. I am striving to be my highest and best self at all times.

I give thanks for the Infinite Healing Presence that is always with me. I give thanks for the wonder and glory of life. **22**

Deep inside me is a wellspring of all good things. Everything I need is within me. God's energy circulating through me, produces my abundance.

God is the never-failing, never-ending Source of all supply. Just as the life circulating within a tree culminates in fruit, so the life circulating within me culminates in the fruits of good action.

23 *Today, I become still inside and touch the Source from which all good things flow.*

God is all Health. God is my health. God is the Supplier of all good things. I am in a prosperous state of consciousness as long as I am attuned to God.

24 *Quietly, I go inward to the source of all abundance, of all power, of all good.* I have more than enough to meet all of my requirements. The energy of life is flowing into me and producing harmony in my world.

I am filled with health. I am filled with a sense of well-being. I am well-adjusted mentally, emotionally and physically.

I affirm prosperity as a permanent part of my life.

....

I share my good with others in whatever I do and wherever I go. I have the consciousness of plenty today. Abundance is everywhere in my world. 25

I draw deeply upon the inner resources of the Spirit. I am one with all that is. All good is flowing into my life from the One Source.

....

Thank You, God, for the abundance which is mine. Thank You for the abundance of my health. I am a whole person. Thank You for the abundance of my happiness. I am a balanced and adjusted person. Thank You for the abundance of my success. 26

I am fulfilled by my work and my relationships. There is no lack anywhere. My mind is filled with God.

27 *I sing with joy and exultation!* There is so much to live for and so much to be thankful for. Thank You, God, for the abundance which is mine.

Today, I focus my attention upon the Infinite Abundance of God. All that God has is mine. My every thought is of plenty and good.

I have an abundance of love in my heart. I have an abundance of ideas in my mind. I have an abundance of energy flowing through my body and soul.

I am thankful for the richness of life.

28 *The energy of the Spirit is enriching my life today and every day.* I am a prosperous person on every level. I am physically and materially healthy. I have all that I need to meet all of my requirements.

I experience the free, full, flow of life on every level. I express my full potential in everything I do.

....

....

....

....

....

....

....

....

....

....

....

29

I am grateful for great blessings from God. I am grateful for life, for love, for wisdom. I give thanks for the privilege of living, of loving, of learning, of growing.

As I go through life, I am gaining a wealth of experience. I am learning the spiritual lessons of peace, love, understanding and discipline. Every day, I am getting closer to the realization of my perfect self.

....

....

....

....

....

....

....

....

....

....

....

30

I am prosperous through my loving attitude toward myself and all others. Out of my love and kindness flows all good into my life.

I live richly in the present moment. I relish life.

I surrender all the unworthy things that I may have been or experienced in the past. I bury the dead past. I release all second-rate, inferior thoughts and feelings.

I transcend to the realm of Infinite Life and Infinite Power. I begin a new life of unprecedented success and prosperity.

May

▪ L I G H T ▪

LIVING LIGHT

As I attune myself to the Inner Life, my awareness expands and I am filled with Perfect Light. I see only bright, beautiful, wonderful Light all around me.

I live this day in the focus of Light. I expect all good things to take place and I know that they do. I am guided in everything that I do. I am always attuned to the wonder and beauty of the Infinite.

Thank You, God, for Your Living Light circulating through me. Thank You for Your Healing Power making me whole. Thank You for the strength and the wisdom within me.

Thank You for Your Protection. I know that there is That within me which is greater than that which is in the world. Only good can come my way.

I am one with Living Light.

Thank You, God, for the Living Light that shines through me now. In the consciousness of Light, I go forward into my day filled with confidence and joy. There is peace in my mind, love in my heart, purity in my soul. I am connected to all that is bright and beautiful and good.

Today, I let my consciousness open up to a higher level of awareness. Divine Light shines through, illuminating all of the dark places and healing all pain.

1

God's Light guides me everywhere I go and in all that I do. I am filled with purpose and vision.

I live from my inner center and listen carefully to my inner wisdom. In the presence of Light, I become still and all of my prayers are answered.

2

3 ***Thank You, God, for the Light that surrounds me.*** Thank You for the Light that fills me with life, love, peace and joy.

As I walk in the Light, today, I am filled with God's Infinite Wisdom. I am filled with Light. The Light within me is my life. The Light within me is the love that I feel for all people.

4 ***My whole body is filled with energy and life.*** I am strong. I am vital. I am whole. I am at peace. I am in tune with the Infinite Light that surrounds me.

I see the One Light today. I open my mind to the light of Truth. I open my heart to the light of love. I open my body to the light of health. I open my world to the light of harmony.

The Spirit within is the Light upon my path.

The Light from above fills me with spiritual understanding and vision. My focus is single and my body is filled with Light. I am a child of Light. I walk in Light.

As Light surrounds me, I am transformed into a new creature. Old, tired energy becomes renewed strength within my mind, my heart and my body.

5

Light rays out from my eyes, from my voice, from my face, from my whole being. I spread Light in everything that I say and do. I surround everyone around me with Light.

I am made whole in the Light. The energy of the Spirit scintillates through my being, today, healing me. I am lifted above the mortal sway.

The Light reveals my innate Divinity. The Light shows me my Infinite Potential. I put myself in God's Hands of Light today.

6

7 *God is the Light that brings all things together and maintains order and harmony in this great, beautiful world.* I experience Living Light in my world today.

I walk in Light today and every day. I am a child of Light. I am created from Light and I am filled with Light. Light flows into me from the Infinite Source.

8 *The Spirit is Light, life is Light, I am Light.* The bright, shining essence of Eternal Life illuminates my mind, my heart, my body and my soul.

Light vibrations enliven my body and make me whole, strong and pure. Light enlivens my mind so that I may think clearly. My heart is filled with warmth and peace.

Quietly, as I dwell at the center of warmth, the energy of the Infinite flows out, becoming all good things in my life.

I give thanks for Truth. I know it, I feel it, I accept it.

9

I live in the Light, today, and all is well. I move in the consciousness of Light today. I am attuned to the inner vibration. God is the One Reality in my life.

As I feel the consciousness of oneness, all lesser things disappear from my life.

The Infinite Healing Presence is flowing through me and revitalizing me. I am sustained by an unfaltering trust. I feel the consciousness of the Presence at all times.

10

I embrace the Light today. I see Light everywhere and in everyone. I become still and I know that all within me is bright, shining and vibrant.

11 ***Thank You, God, for Right Action in my life.*** Thank You for safety and protection. Thank You for the Living Light that guides me through all of my endeavors.

Deep at the center of my being is Perfection. Deep within me is beautiful Light.

12 ***I release myself completely to my inner Perfection.*** I release myself to the oneness of life. Vibrant Light shines through me, making me whole and connecting me to perfect beingness. I release myself to the Divine Light today.

This is my time of prayer. This is my time of inner revelation. This is my time of Light in action in my life.

I keep focused on the realization that the Infinite Presence is with me at all times. I am strengthened and uplifted by this knowledge.

I walk in the Light today. I transcend all external activities, details and difficulties in the presence of the Light.

I live in the consciousness of the One Presence and the One Power. I am confident that God is with me always. I am an open channel through which God's Good flows into my life.

13

Today, I dwell in the Light. Energy is vibrating around me, making me whole, strong and pure. I am attuned to the bright, shining Light of the Spirit. The energy of the universe is within me.

Bright Light illuminates all of the darkness in my mind, my body and my soul, and dissolves all of the pain and doubt.

14

15 *I am a shining example for all to follow.* As I walk in the Light, I am uplifted, cleansed and made whole. I am poised and centered and nothing can disturb the serenity of my soul.

Vibrant energy radiates through every part of my being. I am attuned and aligned. I am regenerated in the consciousness of complete and perfect oneness.

16 *When I am centered, Right Action prevails in all that I do.* I go calmly forward into each day filled with confidence, love and joy.

Divine Light shines in and heals me. I am strong and vital in my oneness with God. I give thanks for the abundance which is mine. I praise God from whom all blessings flow.

A great sense of well-being floods into my being. I am attuned to the bright and beautiful Light. This is a day of Light.

Thank You, God, for this day and the privilege of living it. Thank You for the Light that shines through me and for Your Infinite Healing Presence that indwells me.

Light permeates my mind, heart, soul and body. I am calm, cool and collected. I am peaceful within my being. My consciousness is free.

17

In the Light, I am filled with strength and purpose. I receive inspiration and guidance today, in all of my endeavors.

Everything is fresh and bright today. Every ending is a new beginning.

I am aligned with all that is beautiful and good. I give thanks for God's Blessings which sustain me.

18

19 *The beautiful, bright expression of the Living Light shines through my heart, my mind, my soul and my body today.* I feel Light moving through me, enriching me, uplifting me, sustaining the flow of life at full tide within me.

I give thanks for the wonder and glory of life. I give thanks for the privilege of living life fully and abundantly every day.

20 *I shall not want for anything because the Lord is my Shepherd.* God is the Light shining through my being. I am fulfilled in the Light today.

I cease my labors in the outer world and I go to the Secret Place of the Most High. I find there, love, beauty and joy.

I surround all of my loved ones with protective Light. I have faith that God goes before me making the crooked places straight. I may stumble, but I will never fall. I may grow weary, but I will never faint.

In the consciousness of Light, I have the strength to sustain myself throughout each day, each week, each month, each year, each lifetime throughout Eternity. Light fills my heart. Eternal Life circulates through my being.

    Light is everywhere. The Light shining from above blesses my life. I let my Light shine through today.

21

I love life and I love to live. I live in the Light. I live in Truth. I live in the awareness of One Life.

    The Love of God enlivens me, heals me, blesses me. I am filled with love—love for life, love for God, love for myself, love for my fellow human beings, love for every living creature.

22

23 *I go forward into this day to do that which God has given me to do, filled with Light, love, peace and joy.* All good things come my way.

I walk in the Light, today—the Light of pure Spirit, the Energy of God, the visible form of the Infinite Reality.

I revel in the Light. I give thanks for God's Light with me at all times. I am protected by the Everlasting Arms.

24 *Thank You, God, for Your Power and Your Light today and every day.*

I dwell in the Light—the Light of God's Truth, the Light of God's Energy, the Light of God's Presence. This Infinite Light penetrates every part of my being, my home, my world.

I am one with the Infinite Invisible Reality. 25

Divine Light surrounds and protects me. I am filled with a sense of well-being and warmth. I know that God's Love is all that I need.

The Light of God protects me from any evil that may come my way. No evil shall come near my dwelling place because I am attuned to Light.

The Light of God penetrates my being in bright, beautiful and wonderful ways. I give thanks for 26 the protective Light of God. I know that all is well in my life, today.

My eye is single in its focus on the Light. I am attuned to the Spirit, to the Infinite Life Vibration. I am a child of Light. I walk in Light.

Light surrounds me and transforms me into a new person. I am revitalized in body, spirit, heart and mind. New vitality shows through in everything I do.

27 **Light rays forth from my whole being today.** In everything that I say and do, I am Light. The Light of pure Spirit shines through my being.

Deep within, I experience the Reality of the Divine Presence. I am made whole in God, in Whom I live and move. I wholly devote myself to my higher consciousness.

I am attuned to the universal vibration of Light.

28 **Thank You, God, for my consciousness of Light.** Today, I focus my attention upon Light. I am basking in its warmth and purity.

As I pray, the Light of God flows out and blesses every part of my being. My mind is blessed with Truth. My heart is blessed with love. My body is blessed with health. I am grateful for these great blessings.

I am blessed with good friends and family, expressions of God in my life. God blesses me with everything I need to live a full, vibrant life. 29

From this second onward, I devote my entire life, my entire attention, my entire awareness to the expression of God's Will. I know there is a Light upon my path. I am attuned to the Living Essence within.

God's Protective Light enfolds me and all other people on earth. All things work for good today and always. Thank You, God, for the abundant good in my life. Thank You for my enlightenment. 30

Thank You for this great, beautiful world in which I live. Thank You for the universe. Thank You for the solar system. Thank You for the heavens.

Thank You for the great human family and our shared consciousness of Light.

31

I am thankful for the Divine Light which guides me in the direction I need to go to realize my highest potential.

Today, I become still and pursue the inner quest of total enlightenment. I penetrate into the deep inner mysteries of life. I experience wonders greater than anything that exists in the outer world.

Quietly and calmly, I move toward the Light at the center of my being. There, the Presence of God awaits me—bright, beautiful, loving, kind, gentle and all-embracing.

I am one with God. I am sustained and supported by His Everlasting Arms. I rest in the Rock of Ages.

....

....

....

....

....

....

....

....

....

....

....

....

....

....

....

....

....

....

....

....

June

▪ W I S D O M ▪

I EXPERIENCE SILENT INNER WISDOM

*C**alm, silent, inner wisdom.*** I am attuned to the inner center of wisdom and strength. Nothing can disturb the serenity of my soul.

I experience an understanding greater than all of the knowledge in the world. I know that That which is within me is greater than that which is in the world. For this awareness, I am grateful.

Nothing can come up that God and I together cannot handle. There are no challenges that I cannot meet. I have all the wisdom I need to succeed.

I feel Divine Energy moving through my being today. I feel the Presence of God filling me. The vibrations within me are heightened and quickened. I vibrate in tune with the Eternal Reality.

My mind is clear, my eye is single in its focus and my whole being is filled with Truth.

My eyes are open, today, to Truth, to the wonder and beauty of the inner Life of God. My eyes are open to the beauty in other people. My eyes are open to the love that is being expressed everywhere. My eyes are open to the Truth in all living things.

1

I am attuned to a knowledge which is greater than I am. My eyes are open and I truly see. I see myself as a child of God. I see all others as my brothers and sisters. I see all life as an expression of praise to the Most High.

Calm is established in the center of my being. I am at peace. I know profound experience.

2

Quietly and steadily, I travel to a higher level of spiritual awareness and understanding. I seek the Kingdom of God and all other things are added unto me. I think clearly and positively. Divine Wisdom is mine today.

3 ***Silent, inner knowing unfolds in my consciousness.*** All good unfolds in my world. I am inwardly secure.

I feel peace because the turbulence of the outer world has no effect upon me. I practice non-reaction. All things are possible to him who can perfectly practice non-reaction.

I go into my closet and close the door, and the serene way of the Infinite reveals Itself to me.

4 ***This is my time for practicing my oneness with God.*** I go within and make contact with the Divine Spark, the Light that lighteth the way for every man that cometh into the world.

My consciousness is filled with wisdom. The Divine Spark is ignited within me today.

_____
_____
_____
_____
_____
_____
_____
_____
_____
_____
_____

There is That which goes before me making the crooked places straight. There is That which lifts me to greater heights, inspiring me and bringing me great wisdom.

5

As I am attuned to the Infinite Presence, the Presence is attuned to me. I am an open channel and expression of all that God is.

_____
_____
_____
_____
_____
_____
_____
_____
_____
_____
_____

I feel the full expression of Spirit in my life today.

6

The tide of Infinite Life is surging through me. I see Infinite Abundance everywhere in my world.

I am filled with God and I am filled with Truth. I am grateful for the good unfolding through me now.

7 ***Wherever I am, God's Presence is with me.*** God is all of me. I am that part of God which I can understand.

There is only Perfect God, perfect man, perfect being. Today, I feel the intelligent, all-knowing Energy of God flowing through my being.

I am the complete expression of God today.

8 ***I go forward into this day filled with Divine Wisdom.*** I know that nothing can come up that God and I cannot handle.

I am filled with the Power of the One. God's Wisdom manifests in me as intuition and insight.

With the Wisdom of God, there is no challenge, no difficulty, no obstacle that I cannot overcome.

I am vitalized by the Spirit. I am attuned with gratitude and joy to the Kingdom within me.

9

Divine Light vibrates through me, moving me to a higher level of consciousness. I feel the free, full flow of life surging through me on every level. I am attuned to all that God is. I am one with the Truth.

This is my time of prayer, of inner knowing, of realization. Through prayer, I have been shown the One Perfect Life. This life is my life now.

10

Poised and centered in spiritual consciousness, I know that nothing can disturb the serenity of my soul.

In the blessed quiet, I feel the Presence of the Indwelling Spirit and I give thanks.

11 *I experience perfect awareness and knowing today.* I express every action, every thought and every feeling in the consciousness of Truth. This is a beautiful day, a wonderful life, and it is a great experience just to be alive.

There is That within me which is greater than that which is in the world. There is That which loves me better than I love myself.

God makes me whole with His Infinite Wisdom.

12 *The Infinite Healing Presence is flowing through my being.* Whatever my need, it is met. Wherever there may be pain or congestion, it is dissolved. God is All-knowing.

I am in tune and I know Infinite Truth. Through my quest for inner realization, all good unfolds in me.

Quietly now, I go straight to the center and find there all that is wise, beautiful and good. 13

Through my prayer and meditation, I find understanding, awareness and intuition. All life unfolds from the center of inner knowing.

Thank You, God, for the privilege of oneness with You today.

This is a wonderful day to live, to learn, to grow and to know. I think about my purpose in life. I am clear in what I am here to do. I know who I am. I know where I am going. 14

Through Divine Enlightenment, I know my purpose in life—to live as an expression of the Spirit within and to share my good with others.

15 *I experience my life purpose today.* All that is bright, beautiful and good is projected from me. I am in tune with life and life is in tune with me. The vibrant energy of the Spirit flows through my being on every level.

I am expressing the Truth in all that I do and in all that I am. This is my purpose. I give thanks that this is so.

16 *I am in the fourth dimension where I see and feel things that transcend ordinary life.* My mind is expanding to a new level of awareness.

There are bodies terrestrial and bodies celestial. We have bodies within bodies into Eternity— an infinite number of levels of expression.

I dwell in the fourth dimension. I awaken to a new height of experience, to a greater understanding of my beingness.

17

I am attuned and alert. The Energy of God is pulsating through every cell of my body and I am becoming that Energy.

I dwell upon the larger scope of life. I muse about my relationship to the universe and the wonder of God's Creation. Unseen forces are at work in my life. Although I do not know what lies ahead, I know it will be good.

18

Through prayer, my mind is cleansed. I empty out all distracting thoughts to make room for God.

Thank You, God, for blessing me with Your Wisdom. Thank You, God, for the beauty and richness of Your Life.

19 ***I am one with the Invisible Infinite Essence of all being today.*** I am a channel through which the Infinite Wisdom of God flows forth into expression. I make myself a whole channel by keeping my thoughts clear, my emotions balanced and my body healthy.

Life is a glorious adventure and an opportunity to learn and to grow.

20 ***I am made of a Sublime Essence.*** I am made in the image and likeness of God. There is no limit to my potential, to my prosperity.

I am filled with a sense of wholeness and oneness. I am attuned to the Infinite Source. I go constantly back to the Inner Realm of all understanding.

I affirm safety and guidance in the world today. **21**
Good is unfolding in the lives of people everywhere. Everyone upon the highways, the sky-
ways, the roads, the streets and the bodies of
water is guided and protected.

The Wisdom and Love of God surrounds all.
He is ever present.

Infinite Wisdom flows through me today. I am **22**
the channel through which Truth is expressed.

Divine Inspiration unfolds in my life and I
have more than enough to meet all of my requirements. I have an abundance of creative ideas
with which to realize my goals.

I am prosperous spiritually, mentally, emotionally, physically and materially.

23 *I become still and contemplate the nature of expression and creativity.* I thank God for the opportunity to create and to express.

I thank God for the expression of creative energy in my occupational life and in my personal life. Through Divine Inspiration, I can do anything and I can realize any dream.

24 *Thank You, God, for this day of increased awareness.* Thank You for the privilege of dwelling in Your All-knowing Presence.

Thank You for the privilege of learning and growing. Thank You for challenges through which I can put into practice what I have learned.

Thank You for the courage to face all situations, whatsoever they may be, and for the mighty wisdom to do those things which are to be done by me today.

Thank You for Your Work to do.

Today, I see myself at my highest and best, at all times and in all ways. I go forward into my day secure in the knowledge that God is with me. God is my Supply. God is the Source of all wisdom.

Nothing can disturb the calm serenity of my soul. I work from this inner center of awareness today and always.

25

This is a day of awareness. This is a day of experience.

I have decided to do those things which bring increased awareness into my life and into the lives of everyone I touch. I have decided to make the most of my experiences.

I keep always before me the image of that which I determine to be—a perfect child of God. I express the best I can be at all times.

26

27 ***Ever onward and upward I go into the Light.*** I am realizing my perfect self.

As I move away from the world outside me, desire, urges and appetites dissolve. I move into the Divine Mind and make my decisions and choices from there.

I learn the lessons of spiritual awareness as I become one with the Spirit.

28 ***I am centered in the Spirit today.*** I am centered in Infinite Awareness.

Great Truth is everywhere visible in my world. Harmony flows through me. I am spiritually prosperous. I am aware of my true potential. I have great wisdom.

....
....
....
....
....
....
....
....
....
....
....

Today, I am grateful for my awareness, my perception, my vision given to me by God. **29**

From my center, creativity and inspiration unfold into beautiful works, creations and accomplishments.

Thank You, God, for blessing me with creative power.

....
....
....
....
....
....
....
....
....
....
....

I have the wisdom I need to handle every situation presented to me. **30**

I am thankful for the opportunity to grow and to learn.

I go forward into my day with new ideas and new energy to put to good use. My wisdom and strength are converted into creative, successful works.

I am a successful person, because I am doing God's Work. His Energy and His Wisdom propel me through life.

Monthly Goals

July

▪ W H O L E N E S S ▪

I LIVE LIFE WHOLLY TODAY

My prayer, today, is to realize the Infinite Potential of my life. There is That within me which is greater than that which is in the world. There is That within me which goes before me making the crooked places straight.

In my oneness and in my wholeness, the energy of the Spirit surrounds me, blesses me, heals, sustains and maintains me in the consciousness of abundant life. I am a living expression of God.

I live life wholly today. Health is abounding in me. Life is in free, full flow through me. I experience perfect circulation in my mind, in my heart, in my soul and in my body. I experience perfect health in every part of my being.

I am whole because I am expressing the holiness, the oneness, the completeness, the perfection which is God. I am realizing my full potential.

This is my time of meditation upon health. God is all Health. God is my health. I experience wholeness in my being and in my world of affairs.

I am made whole and strong. My health is the expression of spiritual wholeness in my being. My health is a positive state of mind. I am healthy in every cell of my body, in every nuance of my thought, in every vibration of my being.

1

I affirm my wholeness. I am a whole person in soul, mind, body and world of affairs. All of my parts are integrated and attuned. I contemplate life from the highest level of awareness.

I move upward and inward into union with the universal Presence of the Spirit.

2

3 **In the blessed quietness, I feel a deep sense of well-being.** The Infinite Power of God is present and active in my life and in all of my affairs.

Today, I develop a holistic consciousness. I am made whole by the healing power of Divine Light. I am sustained and comforted in this consciousness of Light. I experience perfect circulation, perfect assimilation, and perfect elimination in my whole body.

4 **I feel the uplifting energy of Light within me.** I feel strength in my entire being. I am a whole person, a vital person, a strong person.

As I dwell in the Light, God moves through me and does His Work. I am an open channel through which His Spirit manifests. I give thanks that this is so.

Today, I think of myself in new and expanded terms. I have unlimited health and prosperity within me. If I am just a little lower than the angels, if I am crowned with honor and glory, then I must be very special. 5

I think of myself as a point of light within the Mind of God, a point of love within the Heart of God, a point of animation within the Body of God. All that He has is expressed through me at every moment. I am a complete expression of Him.

I am a whole person. I am a strong person. I am a successful person. I am joyously attuned to all life in the universe. 6

Thank You, God, for Your Divine Expression manifesting in me. Thank You for Your healing, cleansing, renewing Energy in my life and in my world.

7 *I am renewed.* I am refilled. I am re-energized. I express perfect health. I am strong and vital. My thoughts are clear, my consciousness is pure, my heart is loving.

I open myself to new vistas of human potential. I open myself to Divine Expression.

I am a whole and complete person, today, in my closeness to God.

8 *Today, I have a healthy self-concept.* I conceive of myself as a perfect child of God. This is the premise with which I go forward into my life.

Thank You, God, for the complete and perfect expression of my life. I see myself as prosperous and successful on every level. I am in harmony with the perfect pattern of my perfect self.

I do the best that I am capable of and then I put my trust in God. I trust that the perfect plan is unfolding for me.

_____
_____
_____
_____
_____
_____
_____
_____
_____
_____
_____
_____

9 *Quietly now, I go to the center of my being.* There, I make contact with my Infinite Wholeness. I am one with God's Oneness. His healing Presence is surging through my being, uplifting me, enlivening me, and making me whole.

God's Vitality is in every part of my being and in my world of affairs. I see the Infinite Perfection of the universe duplicated in every aspect of my being.

_____
_____
_____
_____
_____
_____
_____
_____
_____
_____
_____
_____

10 *I am a whole and complete being.* I am made in the image and likeness of God. I am perfect, even as God is Perfect.

I am blessed with perfect circulation in my body and in my entire life. I am attuned to vital, whole, Divine Energy. I am attuned to the right and good path.

I give thanks for my health and for the abundance of good in my life.

11 **Today, my inner confidence leads to success.** My prevailing mental and emotional attitude shapes my outer experience.

Filled with health, joy, enthusiasm, and confidence today, I know I can do that which God has given me to do.

My success is manifesting in my physical health, my emotional balance, and my clear and inspired thinking. I am complete in every part of my life.

I am whole spiritually, strengthened in God's Healing Presence.

12 **In the center of my being, I build a cathedral out of strength, faith, peace, order, and harmony.** I am rich in the materials I need to construct my place of worship.

I have a consciousness of health today. If my consciousness is whole, then my mind, soul and body are also. All good flows into my being. God knows what things I have need of before I ask Him.

I am healthy and happy. I give thanks for the bright beautiful energy vibrating through me on every level.

The abundant flow of God's Health is surging through my body, invigorating me and making me a whole, perfect image of Himself. 13

I feel the inner Presence in every cell of my body. My heart is beating in tune with the rhythm of the universe. My blood stream carries Infinite Life through every organ of my body. I am a new person. I am reborn into Eternal Life. I live forever, every day.

God is all Health. God is the Source of my health. God is every healthy cell of my body. God is my wholesome blood stream. As I accept these truths with conviction, they become my reality. My belief produces my physical health. 14

I am a healthy person now.

15 *I take good care of my body, today, for it is my temple.* I open my body up and let universal perfection, order and harmony flow through. I dwell in the healing Presence of the One.

My body is a temple of purity, strength and vitality. I give thanks for my body now. I give thanks that I am made in the image and likeness of God.

16 *Today, I determine that I shall have a sound mind in a sound body.* Today, my consciousness is clear. I am filled with whole life. I go into my world today, full of health and ready to do those things which have been assigned for me to do.

I am creative in mind, warm in heart, strong in body, purposeful in action. I give thanks for constructive, joyous, healthy life today.

I am still and dwell in the consciousness of perfect health. No matter what turbulence may arise within me, nothing can disturb the calm of my soul.

I vibrate in tune with the healing power of Light. I am made whole. According to my faith, it is done unto me.

17

The Infinite Healing Presence is doing its work in me today, repairing, healing, and regenerating all the cells of my body. My body is a temple of the Holy Spirit.

I am eternally young. I am eternally alive. This is the first day of the rest of my healthy life. God is all Health. God is my health now.

I whole, vigorous, and vital. I give thanks for my healthy consciousness and my healthy body now.

18

19

I am attuned to healthful vibrations today. I am an outlet of all good, because I have first been an inlet for God's Good. I feel the free, full, flow of life surging through me today. I feel the Healing Presence in my heart, in my mind, in my soul, in my body and in my world of affairs.

God is in His Heaven, and all is right with the world. As I attune my consciousness to the higher vibration within me, I feel goodness in the very cells of my body. My body is a temple of the Living Spirit.

20

Health manifests on the outside when I am healthy on the inside.

Today, I affirm health in my soul. I affirm health in my mind. I affirm health in my body.

I turn my attention towards all that is bright, beautiful and good. I think positively. I live creatively. I feel deeply and fully.

The Spirit is moving through me and blessing me with health in all parts of my being.

Quietly now, I go inward and make contact with the Infinite Healing Presence. There I experience the peace that passeth all understanding.

I believe in the Inner Reality. The Inner Reality is my intuition, awareness, inspiration and insight.

Thank You, God, for my spiritual realization. Thank You for the healing flow of vital energy which strengthens me, uplifts me and sustains me. Thank You for the privilege of experiencing the highest level of expression.

21

In the consciousness of healing, I go forward into this day.

Today, I am whole. Today, I am healed. Today, I am cleansed. Whatever there is in my being that needs attention, I surround it with the pure, healing Light.

The cleansing energy of the Spirit is flowing through every level of my being. I know that a sound mind in a sound body is the way to a sound life. My mind becomes sound as I open it to the Spirit. Pure vibrations heal me and uplift me. I am focused on my good and perfect self.

22

23 *I feel the flow of healing Power washing over me.* It is great just to be alive. There is That within me which loves me better than I love myself.

The Infinite Healing Presence is always with me and never fails me. Whatever my need, it is met. Whatever my pain or congestion, it is dissolved.

I am in tune with the perfect energy of the Infinite and I am healed.

24 *I speak the word of wholeness, today, for myself and for others.*

A whole person is a complete, balanced, mature individual. I endeavor to be complete, balanced and mature at all times.

I keep my words kind, my actions controlled, my body pure, my feelings warm and my thoughts clear.

I feel the creative activity of Divine Mind working through my mind, lifting me to greater levels of awareness and understanding.

I embrace the inner Source of my beingness. 25
God is all Health. God is my health. I revel in my oneness with God.

I am in tune with life and life is in tune with me. I experience perfect circulation, perfect assimilation, perfect elimination in my body.

I am one with the natural forces of life. I am one with all life.

This is a time of calm, silent inner knowing. This 26
is a day of Light, a day of inner worship. I let the Source penetrate through my consciousness. I feel Divine Energy surging through my body.

Tranquil inner experience is mine today. I am aware of the Presence of God within. I am one with the Living Presence.

27 *Eternal Life is resurrecting me today.* I am filled with vibrant energy in every part of my being. I am cleansed, purified, healed.

I am firmly rooted in the consciousness of well-being and oneness. I am experiencing a new, beautiful life.

I give thanks for the Spirit enthroned in my consciousness today and every day.

28 *I am attuned to the Energy of God in every part of my being today.* Peaceful, silent inner knowing flows through me. Divine Order and Right Action unfold in my world because my mind, heart and soul are harmonious and peaceful. I am a whole person. My words are kind. My actions are controlled. My thoughts are clear. My body is pure. My heart is warm.

I express my wholeness at all times in all ways. I do my best to realize my highest good always.

This is a day to be conscious of my mental and emotional attitude. Attitude is everything. Attitude can make the darkest day bright. A cheerful attitude can turn the worst situation around. I have a positive and healthy attitude toward life today.

I have a self fit to live with. I have a philosophy fit to live by. I have a world fit to live in.

I anticipate all impending events with expectation of good. I am on top of things and I feel balanced and whole.

29

Healing depends upon my expanded state of consciousness. Healing depends upon my oneness with the Infinite.

I open myself to the Healing Power by turning away from negative, outer conditions or circumstances, and toward my inner Perfection. I affirm wholeness, balance and order in my life today.

30

31 *I am renewed.* New life surges through me. I am cleansed, strengthened and healed.

Attunement to God requires all of my concentration and energy. But, although it is a demanding endeavor, the rewards are great. I am blessed with a tremendous sense of well-being and joy as I move through the days of my life doing those things which God has given me to do. In my connection to God, I feel great confidence and meaning in my life.

Never before have I felt anything like the great, uplifting inspiration I experience in the Presence of God. I will dwell in the Inner Reality all the days of my life.

Monthly Goals

_____
_____
_____
_____
_____
_____
_____
_____
_____
_____
_____
_____
_____
_____
_____
_____
_____
_____
_____
_____
_____
_____

August

▪ F A I T H ▪

I EXPERIENCE THE PRESENCE IN PRAYER

I *dwell in the consciousness of faith.* The energy of the Spirit is permeating my thoughts, feelings, actions—all that I am.

Thank You, God, for the privilege of faith. Thank You for the privilege of prayer. Thank You for the privilege of sharing. Thank You for the Light that moves through my being. Thank You for understanding.

I live, today, in the consciousness of the Spirit. I live in the consciousness of the One. Thank You, God, for the living beauty of life. I am grateful for all that You are, for all that life is and for all that I can be.

I live from the center of my being. The spiritual energy I feel in worship and prayer, makes me strong and whole. I cooperate by taking care of my body and by taking care of my mind. I nurture my body and my mind with positive thoughts and feelings.

Thank You, God, for Your Presence with me at all times.

Today, I go forward in faith. Faith is believing in yourself, believing in life, believing in God, believing in other people and believing in what you are doing. Faith is a spiritual, mental, and emotional attitude that cannot conceive of its opposite.

My strong faith is the assurance of my success and prosperity. I have faith in the unfolding of all good in me. I give thanks for complete faith today.

1

All fear is dissolved from my consciousness. All anxiety, tension, pressure and confusion are dissolved, and replaced by Divine Faith.

Deep, vital faith is established in my consciousness. I am sustained by unfaltering trust.

There is a river which flows through and nourishes me. The river carries me toward my oneness with God, toward the Truth, toward my freedom.

2

3 *I am filled with a strong faith today.* Faith is an affirmative attitude. God's Faith is within me and I am strengthened mentally, emotionally and spiritually. My consciousness is attuned.

I am filled with assurance and confidence. My faith makes me so. My faith springs up into Everlasting Life. My faith can move mountains.

Bob

4 *My faith is based on the understanding that God is the One Power in my life.* My faith springs out of God's Love in my life.

Today, I go forward with a strong and steadfast faith to do those things that God has given me to do. All fear is dissolved on every level. There is no uncertainty, no sense of trepidation.

I am filled with abundant faith today.

I am strong and steadfast in my faith. I am one
with God. All of the good of the Kingdom is mine
at all times and in all ways. My faith makes me
whole. My faith is the healing energy of the Spirit
blessing my body, my mind, my heart, my world
of affairs.

I give thanks for faith. I not only have faith in
God, I have the Faith of God. This faith gives me
the assurance I need today.

5

**This is a day of worship, a day of knowing, a
day to be still.**

Deep at the center of my being, I find
Perfection. Deep within, I find Light.

I release myself completely to my Perfection—God within me. I release myself to my oneness with Him.

The free, full flow of life surges through me,
making me a whole, perfect being.

6

7 *I am filled with the strength of my faith today.* I have faith in God, faith in life, faith in other people. I have faith in Divine Order and Right Action unfolding in everything that I do. I have faith in my goodness and my success. I have faith in me.

Faith is the strengthening, vitalizing activity of my life. Faith gives me the strength I need to go forward, today, to do the things which are to be done by me.

My faith is my positive statement toward life.

8 *All beautiful and wonderful things take place in my life today.*

My faith is strong and ever present. I sustain a positive attitude at all times no matter what comes my way.

I have faith that my body is strong and healthy. I have faith that my mind is clear. I have faith that my heart is warm. I have faith that I can realize all of my dreams.

....
....
....
....
....
....
....
....
....
....
....

Free from all fear, I express faith in everything I do, feel and think. I am an open channel through which the Infinite Abundance of the universe flows out. **9**

I have faith that the Law of Abundance is at work in my life. Through living faith, my understanding and awareness grow greater. The free, full, flow of life surges through me and abundance manifests in every part of my life. I give thanks that this is so.

....
....
....
....
....
....
....
....
....
....
....

Today, I am anchored in a strong and steadfast faith. My faith is the spiritual conviction that there is One Presence and One Power in the universe, present and active in my life and in all of my affairs. **10**

I live my life entrenched in mighty faith. My faith blesses me with all good things in my life and I share my good fortune with others.

11 ***The Lord is my Shepherd, I shall not want.***
What a great statement of assurance! How wonderful it is to know that when I am with God, He looks after me and I shall never want for anything. Therefore, I am already prosperous. I am filled with the wealth of the Kingdom, because the Lord is my Shepherd.

God has had His Arms around me for a long time and He's not going to ever take them away. I stay close to my inner center of support. I am replenished and uplifted by God's Infinite Presence in my life.

12 ***Today, I dissolve all fear.*** I look at all fear that may be lurking within me, and I say, "You are nothing trying to be something. You have no place in my life. Therefore, I dissolve you." I am free from fear because I am filled with faith.

Faith is a positive mental, emotional and spiritual attitude which cannot conceive of its opposite. I have faith in life, faith in God, faith in myself, and faith in my fellow brothers and sisters in this great world. I have faith that everything is working for the ultimate good of all.

I have a grateful consciousness today. I give thanks for this day. God is blessing me. God is blessing this day. God is blessing all my fellow human beings whom I meet along the way in the glorious adventure of life.

I know that only good can come to me, today, because there is only good in my heart, only good in my mind, only good in my soul.

I have faith in meditation as the way to abundant life. I give thanks that this is so.

13

I am filled with abundant life today. Each time I go to my inner center, I am lifted to a new height of consciousness and experience.

All good flows into my life today. I draw to me that which God has given me. I draw to me all that I need for my full and complete experience. I have faith in my ability to achieve my goals.

14

15 *I believe in resurrection and renewal.* Today, I cleanse my mind, heart and soul of all emotional garbage and negativity. I become free inside. I know the Truth and the Truth makes me free.

Today, I follow the Light. I follow the beam of intuition and inspiration that comes from within.

I remove myself from the trivial concerns of the outer world and focus on the larger scope of life. My consciousness is attuned to a higher vibration. I am a spiral of ascending consciousness now and always.

16 *This is my time of inner contact with the Infinite Source of life.* I praise God from whom all blessings flow.

I dwell in the Infinite Invisible Reality. All of God's Good is flowing into my mind, my heart, my soul, my body. As I experience inner abundance, it expresses outwardly in my world.

I am secure in the assurance of God's Love.

I dedicate myself to God's Work, sharing my love and blessings with all people. I count my blessings today.

Peace on earth is established from the peace within my heart. 17

I send out blessings to all people everywhere, surrounding them with Light so that they may be protected and guided in all that they do.

Divine Love blesses me, heals me and flows out into my world.

I give thanks for people. I give thanks for myself. I give thanks for life. I give thanks for faith.

I give thanks for the challenges that face me today. 18 I give thanks for the opportunity to grow, to learn and to expand.

I go forward into this day, into this week, into this month, into the remainder of this year, filled with the awareness that God within me is greater than any challenge which is in the world.

God is blessing my life. God is blessing my family. God is blessing my work. God is blessing all that I am and all that I have to do.

Every challenge is a blessing today.

19 *My prayer, today, is for Grace.* Grace is the out-pouring of God's Love and Kindness into His Creation. I am blessed with His Grace.

I am the recipient of Grace whether I earn it or not, because God loves me. No matter how far I have strayed, no matter what I have done, God's Love is ever there. His Love is manifested in Grace.

As I draw close to God, the warm embrace of His Love surrounds me with Infinite Blessing and Infinite Grace.

I have faith in God's Grace working for good in my life today.

20 *I am refreshed by the rain from Heaven today.* This is a beautiful, wonderful day to be grateful for. I give thanks for the rain that carries with it life, refreshment, energy, and blessings from God. The wonderful rain nourishes the crops and brings new life to all growing things.

Thank You, God, for the rain. Thank You for the clouds. Thank You for all the growing things. Thank You for all the crawling things. Thank You for people.

All the wonder of God's Earth makes my faith strong.

This is my time of prayer. This is my time of inner contact with the Spirit. I let go of outer concerns and I bring my mind into focus. **21**

All good is unfolding in my life. I seek first inner balance and oneness, and all other things are added unto me.

I have faith in my creative expression now and always.

All of my good comes from the Infinite. I am a channel through which God's Love is expressed. **22**

Life is in free full flow through me. I am a whole person—integrated spiritually, mentally, emotionally and physically.

I am sitting on top of the world today. I act as though I own the earth because I surely do. I am made in the image and likeness of God and have been given dominion over all the world.

23 *I have a strong and vital faith.* The faith which flows through my being strengthens me and uplifts me.

Today, I have the conviction that whatever needs to be done, I can do. Divine Inspiration blesses and increases all good things in my life.

I joyously engage in creative activity each moment of this day. I am successful in all of my undertakings.

24 *Today, I work on my self-confidence.* Self-confidence is the basis for all good. As I grow in assuredness, goodness multiplies in my life.

Deep and abiding faith dissolves all fear. My fear dissolves as soon as I reveal and examine it. What am I afraid of? Nothing! "Fear knocked at the door. Faith answered. No one was there."

I walk steadfastly forward into life filled with confidence and joy. My positive mental attitude and my warm, loving heart begin in faith.

Thank You, God, for the faith that strengthens my life today.

Today, I contemplate my oneness with God. God is all of me. I am that part of God which I can understand. **25**

When I am confronted by a challenge of any kind, I think of God and the challenge—whatever it is—becomes an opportunity. I have faith that God will see me through anything because I am one with Him.

Meditation is the way to great riches and happiness. In meditation, I am freed from old conditioning and false beliefs. A new, harmonious world awaits me within.

Thank You, God, for sustaining faith. Thank You for positive and loving feelings. **26**

Divine Order and Right Action prevail in my world. Everything is unfolding as it should for the betterment of all.

I look out upon my world as monarch of all that I see and experience. I believe I am an expression of God in action. I give thanks for the faith that unites all of us in the human family. I give thanks for the peace on earth which begins with me.

27 *Power comes from being attuned to the Spirit within.*

I learn to use this Power so that I may heal myself and others. I learn from God's Teachings to use this Power wisely and for the benefit of all. With this Power, I can overcome all obstacles in my path.

I learn how to let go and let Power prevail in all of my affairs. My faith in myself is immutable. I have faith in God's Power working for good in my life always.

28 *I forgive myself for all past real or fancied wrongs.* If anyone has wronged me, I forgive them. If I have done wrong, I forgive myself. I free myself from fear and guilt so that I can move forward with strong and vital love. I love life and the privilege of living it. I love other people and the privilege of knowing them. I love myself and my likeness to God. I love my work and the opportunity to express my creativity.

I know that God is Love. I have faith that God loves me and that all is well in my world today.

This is my time of inner prayer, of inner qui- 29
etude, of inner awareness.

Today, I surrender all concern about external things. I am able to look at outer situations and say, "It doesn't matter just because it doesn't matter."

When I am quiet on the inside, the turbulence on the outside subsides. I have faith in Divine Order and Right Action unfolding in my life now and always.

There is One Presence and One Power in the 30
universe, active in my life and in all my affairs.
There is no place where God is not.

There is no place where God leaves off and I begin. We are one. There is only Perfect God, perfect man, perfect being. I have faith that this is so.

I am not just a human being living in this world. I am a spiritual being going through a human experience on the way toward complete and perfect unfoldment.

31

I am established in a strong and steadfast faith. Today, I go forward with great confidence to do those things which are to be done by me. I am filled with the trust that everything will turn out for the best. If at first I am disappointed by an outcome, I reconsider it and I find that I always gain something good from it.

Nothing stands in the way of the realization of my goals. The obstacles that appear to block my way are really helping to guide me in the right direction. I discover good even in things that seem bad or disadvantageous.

I have faith in life, I have faith in myself, I have faith in all that is good. I have faith in Divine Order and Right Action taking place in all the world.

Monthly Goals

_____
_____
_____
_____
_____
_____
_____
_____
_____
_____
_____
_____
_____
_____
_____
_____
_____

September

▪ ATTUNEMENT ▪

I AM IN TUNE WITH THE INFINITE

I **am in tune with the Infinite Invisible Reality at the center of my being.** All happiness, health, prosperity, success, freedom and inspiration come from the Light within, the Light that shines through my being and rays out for all to see.

There is One Presence and One Power in the universe, present and active in my life and in all of my affairs. I am one with God.

My mind is clear, my heart is warm, my consciousness is attuned, my body is vitalized, my world is ordered and balanced and everything unfolds as it should in my life. I expect the best, today, on every level and in every way.

As I go out to greet the day, I give thanks for the great blessings which are mine. I give thanks for the consciousness of the Spirit moving through me.

As I go forward into this day, a feeling of profound oneness is with me every step of the way. My life is God's Life. I am attuned to Him in everything I do.

1

I feel the workings of God in all of my affairs. The Living Light of the Spirit is bringing me into alignment with all that is bright, beautiful and good.

I am one with all wonderful things today. This feeling of oneness sweeps through my entire being, uplifting me, inspiring me and healing me. I share an inner consciousness of the Spirit with all living beings.

2

I am attuned to the universe, to God, and to all beautiful life today.

3 *I feel perfect oneness in my entire life today, and I share this with others.* I look for ways to give. I look for ways to be of greater service.

I am in this world for the purpose of living, loving, learning, growing and becoming a perfect expression of God. All things unfold in perfect order in my life and in the lives of all people in the world.

....
....
....
....
....
....
....
....
....
....

4 *I am attuned to the Infinite Healing Presence within and I live from this reality.* God's Love surrounds me, uplifts me and makes me whole on every level.

There is One Life and this life is mine now. I am grateful for the great spiritual awareness that flows through every part of my being.

....
....
....
....
....
....
....
....
....
....

_____
_____
_____
_____
_____
_____
_____
_____
_____
_____
_____

Today, I go forward, secure in the realization that God is present and active in my life and in all of my affairs. I know that nothing can come up, today, that God and I together cannot handle. 5

We are partners in all things. God working through me, is my strength, my guidance, my inspiration, my very center.

I am sustained and soothed by an unfaltering trust today.

_____
_____
_____
_____
_____
_____
_____
_____
_____
_____
_____

I become still and become one with the universe. I am one with God. I am one with the vast spaces and reaches of Eternity. All life is vibrating through me. 6

All of the abundance of the Infinite Universe is available to me and I claim it today. I claim the wonderful experience of life. I claim all good things for myself and all others.

7 *Serene, I stand in the Presence of the Spirit.* I draw from the heights, the depths and the width of the Spirit all the strength I need.

I revel in the harmonious and joyous experience of my oneness.

God is my close companion, my friend, my mentor, my master, my leader, my teacher, my all. I am one with the goodness and the beauty of His Universe today.

8 *The Will of God is uppermost in my consciousness.* Today, I attune my will to His. My will is the executive power of my mind and it governs the choices I make. I choose to attune my mind to God.

All darkness is dispelled by the Light of the Spirit within me. I see my way clearly. I use my will to focus my attention.

My true nature is Spirit. My true self is the God Self.

> 9

My life is God living His Life through me. I am a perfect child of God. I cannot conceive of myself as anything less.

I release myself from everything into the consciousness of the Spirit. I release myself from everything unlike the Nature of God. I proclaim the Glory of God today.

God lives in my heart today. I am an expression of all that He is. The Living Light of the Spirit scintillates through my being, healing and uplifting me above the mortal sway.

> 10

I recognize my innate Divinity. I recognize my Infinite Possibility. I put myself in God's Hands and I know there is nothing that I cannot accomplish today.

God is the Love that brings all things together and maintains this great and beautiful world in harmony and order.

11   ***In God, I live and move.*** I am connected to the creative Presence. I feel God's Greatness working in my life. I feel Divine Energy in free, full flow through me.

I am a whole and healthy person. I am a bright and beautiful person. I am doing God's Work.

12   ***All goodness is within me.*** I seek first the Kingdom and all other things are added unto me.

I turn within—I go into the closet and close the door to the outside world—and make contact with the Infinite Source.

The Law of Abundance is flowing through me and all good things are expressed in my life on every level.

I know the Truth and this awareness makes me free. From the center of my being, I experience the wholeness and the oneness which is God. My heart bursts with joy in His Healing Presence.

    God's Truth is reflected in my eyes, in my voice, in my mind, in my total awareness, in every bright and beautiful thing in the universe.

13

Quietly now, I go inward. I find there the Source of all Power.

    Any fear I have dissolves before the Presence of God. I am free from apprehension, worry, anxiety, concern. I dwell at the center of deep peace. I have faith in life, faith in good, faith in myself, faith in other people.

    I let my consciousness expand. I place everything lovingly in the Hands of God.

14

15 *I keep focused on my oneness with God today.* I am attuned to the Divine Presence within. I see only that which is wonderful, that which is good in my world.

All is God, all is good, all is well. I live from the inner center from which all of my blessings come. I give thanks for the abundance of good in my life today.

16 *I am in tune with the Infinite Source of life.* My mind is filled with God. My heart is filled with God. My body is filled with His Abundant Energy.

I am a whole person. I experience complete attunement in all of my being. The Spirit of God is expressed in all that I am. The Perfect Self is my self.

17

Quietly and calmly, I travel inward and upward to the Secret Place of the Most High.

Today, I enlist myself in God's Great Cause. He directs me. All parts of my self—my physical self, my emotional self, my mental self, my spiritual self—are attuned to Him.

I am His disciple. I move forward in the path of my life endeavoring to serve, to love and to share.

As I move forward, I give thanks for the wonder and beauty of life.

18

This is a day of release—of letting go of outer concerns and letting God in. I release all things unlike the Nature of God.

This is a blessed day. This is God's Day and I live it fully. I release and relax.

I leave all cares behind. I leave off wondering and pondering. I move into greater understanding where there are no questions, only answers.

19 *Divine Guidance flows through my being today.* Infinite Wisdom indwells me and I know that I am upon the right path.

Today, I am directed and protected in the path of righteousness. I am sustained and maintained in wholeness. I am healthy in all ways.

20 *This is my time of prayer, healing and inner attunement.* I am focused on all that is bright, beautiful and good. I am in tune with life today.

My inner consciousness of wholeness and oneness becomes a living, visible manifestation in my outer self and reality.

I am strong, vital and able to do whatever God has given me to do.

Quietly, in the inner Light, I find the consciousness of the One. I find peace, joy, warmth and love.

I carry this consciousness with me at all times. I know that there is Light with me wherever I am and in whatever I do.

21

Quietly now, I go to the Secret Place of the Most High. Traveling upward and inward, I leave the concerns of the material world way behind.

I bless the parts of my body. Blessed be my head through which I know the Power of God. Blessed be my heart that beats in rhythm with the Heart of the universe.

22

23 *I travel upward and inward through the emotional level of feeling and urge, desire and memory; through the realm of the conscious mind where choices and plans are made, and action initiated; finally arriving at my soul, where peace, spiritual love, understanding, gentleness and purity reign.* I break through to the Universal Reality of the Infinite Self.

In the realm of the Secret Place of the Most High, my eye is single in its focus and my whole body is full of Light. I feel profound oneness.

24 *I have a complete sense of well-being today.* I am attuned to That which is whole within me, and which flows out and expresses wholeness in my world. I am integrated and attuned in soul, mind and body.

God is the Perfection within me. I am sustained by an Infinite Faith in Him.

I see myself as a spiritual being, going through a human, physical experience on the way toward complete and perfect unfoldment of my real self.

....

....

....

....

....

....

....

....

....

....

I am made whole in the image and likeness of God. I am attuned to the wholeness of the universe.

25

My life is fulfilled as I move steadily forward on my inner spiritual path. My life is strong, bright and filled with promise.

I give thanks for the abundance of the Spirit in my life. The Spirit is active, creative and vital within my being.

....

....

....

....

....

....

....

....

....

....

....

....

This is my time of prayer and blessing.

26

Today, I am immortal. I live each moment fully as if it were both my first and my last. I believe in the Infinite Healing Presence that flows through me, uplifts me, heals me, blesses me.

27 *I am lifted up, today, to greater realization of my self.*

I follow God's example in correct thought and correct action. I align myself with His Will and I never deviate.

The entire universe is lifted up—all of its galaxies, its stars, its heavenly bodies, its planets, its spaces—into the realization of God and His Power.

28 *God is the Light and Power in my life.* His constant Presence makes me secure. All lesser things disappear from my life. I am sustained and maintained by an unfaltering trust.

God is the Source of my life, the Source of my supply, the Source of my complete and total good. I give thanks for my attunement to Him today.

I walk with God today. I dwell in the One. His Presence is within me. **29**

I leave all of the situations and circumstances of my life behind and go into the Secret Place of the Most High. I dwell there in serenity and harmony. I experience oneness with God.

I go forward into this day filled with inner peace and order. All good is unfolding in my life as I walk with God today.

In this time of inner attunement, I know that God is my very being. **30**

God lives in my heart and I live in the Heart of God. His love flows out as creative inspiration and action in my life.

Abundant good and harmony unfold in my life. They are evidence of my spiritual wholeness and oneness. I live in a bright and beautiful world.

.... **Monthly Goals** ....
....
....
....
....
....
....
....
....
....
....
....
....
....
....
....
....
....
....
....
....
....
....

October

▪ J O Y ▪

I AM FILLED WITH THE JOY OF LIVING

I *give thanks for the joy of life today.* I give thanks for the wonder of God. I am one with God, one with the universe, one with this great, surging, wonderful tide of Spirit that moves through my being and through all of mankind.

The great mystery and joy of life are mine today. I share this joy of living with all of my human family members. We are united in joy.

As I look for ways to give and to share, my consciousness is enriched. My sharing comes back to me in beautiful ways.

Joy, health, abundance, success, inspiration and love are the wonderful gifts from God which He has made abundant in my world.

Thank You, God, for continual, ever-increasing joy. Today, I am a joyful winner. I am on top of things. There is nothing I cannot do, because with God, all things are possible.

I am one with God. God is all of me. I am that part of God which I can understand. I am a joyful expression of Him.

1

Everything works for good in my life today. I am in tune with the Infinite. I am one with the joyful Spirit and all good is unfolding in my life now. I give thanks that this is so.

This is a beautiful day, a bright day, a wonderful day, a day to rejoice and be glad. This day has been given to me to do wonderful things. This is the first day of the rest of my life.

2

3 **On this beautiful day, I am integrated spiritually, mentally, emotionally and physically.** I express God in every part of my life. In joy, I sing out my praise to God.

I am filled with zeal. Enthusiastically, I bring my creativity into full expression through the work which God has given me to do.

I feel the harmony of the universe in my being and I become one with the perfect movement of the spheres. I am one with all universal Perfection. I am one with beauty and good.

4 **I love life and I love to live.** I am filled with joy. My life comes from God, and, joyfully, I let God express His Will through me in every part of my being.

Joy enlivens my life today. Thank You, God, for this day of Light and joy.

Each moment is blessed. Each activity in which I engage is blessed with joy.

I am light in heart, clear in mind, vital in spirit, healthy in body and whole in my entire being. 5

Joy surges through me, making my life complete. This is a day of joy, health, success and prosperity.

I am grateful for my happiness. My happiness is the Kingdom of God manifesting through me. I seek first the Kingdom of happiness and all other things are added unto me.

God is all Joy. My joy grows out of my oneness with God. I am filled with love and joy, and I give 6 thanks that this is so.

I spread joy in the world today. I express it in my health, my prosperity, my love and my peace. I am a joyous person.

I recognize the Presence of the Indwelling Spirit. It bubbles up within me as joy unrestrained. I anticipate all impending events with enthusiasm and expectation of good. I am filled with joy every step of the way.

7 *My joy affects other people.* It inspires them and uplifts them. There is laughter, gaiety and joy in my world today.

The inner quest beckons me, today, and I pursue it. I penetrate into the deep inner mysteries of life and of God. I am overjoyed by my expanded awareness of life.

The loving, kind, gentle, all-embracing Presence of God awaits me. I am supported by His Everlasting Arms. I place myself joyfully in His Hands.

8 *I am filled with the sweetness of life and I am joyful.* This is my time of meditation upon happiness. I am a happy person. I am in tune with life and life is in tune with me. I seek first the Kingdom and all happiness unfolds in my life in every way.

I feel the free, full, flow of life surging through me, vitalizing me, and making me whole. As I drink of the water that the Spirit gives me, a well of water springs up within me into Everlasting Life.

I experience ecstasy today.

Today is my day. I live it fully. Today, I am on the high road to happiness, health, success and prosperity.

I give thanks for the joy that surges through me on every level. The free, full flow of life is surging through me and making me whole and happy.

9

I am joyful today!

There is One Life and I am living it fully. This life is God's Life expressing itself through me. Whatever I do, today, I find fulfillment.

I am guided by Infinite Intelligence. I am sustained by the creative force of life.

I go forward anticipating all impending events with joy and expectation of good. My health shows it. I am healthy. My attitude shows it. I am positive.

10

11 *I give thanks for joy today and every day of my life.*

Upward and inward I go, today, away from the world around me, into the realm of my mind. As I focus my mind on a single purpose, my body is filled with Light and joy.

I release all worry and pain, and focus on my oneness with God. Light rays into my being, filling me with brightness and beauty.

12 *I am truly a child of God.* I have everything I need to be happy.

The brightness and beauty of life fill my being today. I am in tune with all good. I am aligned with the Divine Forces from above. The Infinite Energy of God flows in, awakening me to higher potential on every level.

_____
_____
_____
_____
_____
_____
_____
_____
_____
_____
_____
_____

As the Light rays into me, I am overwhelmed with joy. There is nothing more sublime than this feeling of harmony. I am cleansed, renewed, healed.

Quietly, I center myself. I experience the consciousness of joy within my being. I am attuned to the Divine Presence, and joy and Light emanate from me.

13

_____
_____
_____
_____
_____
_____
_____
_____
_____
_____
_____

There is only One Life. This life is joyous. This life is my life now.

Quietly, I go to the center of all Power. Energy is flowing into me, taking form and expressing itself in my joy and harmony.

I am filled with joyful health. I am filled with joyful well-being. I am well-adjusted mentally, emotionally and physically.

I am mature and attuned. I feel God's Presence with me at all times, enriching me and uplifting me.

14

15 *I share my joyful good with others in whatever I do and wherever I go.* I experience great pleasure in return. For this I give thanks.

The wonder of being fills me today. I am joyous because I have the conviction that God is within me, strengthening me, protecting me. There is no place where God leaves off and I begin.

I feel the vital activity of pure Spirit moving through me, making me whole and bringing me into full alignment with all the forces of nature.

16 *I am happy and I am whole.* I am complete in every way. I give thanks for my good fortune. I anticipate all impending events with enthusiasm and expectation of good. I am filled with joy. I am filled with Light. I am filled with peace. I spring forth joyfully to do those things which are to be done by me.

Thank You, God, for this day of love, this day bursting forth with joy. Life is a joyous experience in which to learn, to grow and to do all that God has given me to do.

Thank You, God, for the joyous contact with the Spirit. Thank You for centeredness. Thank You for the Living Light in my heart, mind, soul and body.

I am filled with joy and enthusiasm. I may not know what's ahead for me today, but I know it can only be good.

Today, I am in tune with the Infinite. Today, I am joyful, I am strong, I am whole, I am new.

17

I give thanks for the abundance that is mine. I give thanks for the Infinite Spirit which uplifts, heals and blesses me.

Today, I am afire with the wonder and the beauty of life. I am joyous. I am filled with the Light of the Holy Spirit.

This Light shines upon my path. It illuminates all of the dark places. It directs me towards my highest good.

18

19 *I am a native of Eternity. I am a child of Light. I* move joyously forward into this sunny, new day. Joyously I live in the consciousness of the Light. The joy of living inundates me today.

Thank You, God, for this day of joy. Thank You for the opportunity to express health, happiness and freedom at all times.

Joy cometh in the morning of my awakening to new and vital experience. Joy permeates my thoughts, warms my heart, and uplifts my spirit. All good and wonderful things are expressed in joy.

20 *Thank You, God, for the joy in my life today.*
I determine to keep my mind clear, my heart joyful, my body pure, my actions controlled and my words kind. I exist on all of these levels simultaneously. My heart rules my outer world, my mind rules my inner world.

The Spirit within enlivens me and I am a joyful expression of It.

Today, I am happy, whole and sound because I maintain constant contact with God. **21**

I am one with God today. I am one with the universe in all of its beauty and all of its joy. Infinite Life is taking place within and through me now. I am in tune with the Infinite.

All things are good and beautiful in the natural order of life. I dissolve all false beliefs in my heart, in my mind and in my soul. I attune my consciousness to the smiling repose of the Infinite.

I go forward into this day joyfully and expectantly, filled with a sense of meaning. All things **22** unfold perfectly, for God is the core of my being.

This is a day of joy, a day of success, a day of unfoldment.

I give thanks for abundance of supply, abundance of happiness, abundance of health, abundance of freedom, abundance of creativity. There is abundance everywhere in my world. I give thanks for the free, full, flow of joyous life.

23 **I am part of this great, unfolding, joyful universe.** Today, I give thanks for the privilege of participating in the great panorama of life. I give thanks for the joy of living. I give thanks for the experience of joyful life today. This is a time of awakening.

Thank You, God, for the abundance of joy which is mine. Thank You for the love everywhere in my world. Thank You for a beautiful life to enjoy.

From my sense of inner well-being, I realize new potential today. I experience all that is whole and good.

24 **I am attuned to greater potential.** I am attuned to my true self. For this I am grateful and joyful.

As I travel to the center of my being, I find there a wellspring of joy bubbling up into expression of all good.

Joyously I celebrate my worthiness. I take pride in my worthy ideas. I thank God for joyful inspiration.

I anticipate all impending events with enthusiasm and expectation of good. I sing with joy and exultation! Deep at the center of my being, I feel the Presence of God. I am attuned to the joy of the universe.

25

God's Life is manifesting through me now. I am one with all that is bright, beautiful and good. I am an expression of God, made in His image and likeness. In this understanding, I awaken to new and Infinite Potential.

All good is unfolding in my life as health, happiness, prosperity, success, freedom, love, creative self-expression. This is a beautiful day of joy, a beautiful day to grow, to know, to worship.

26

I give thanks for this day. I give thanks for this opportunity to live. I give thanks for the joy present in every part of my life.

I am attuned to the greatness of the Spirit and I know that all is well. I have a deep sense of inner peace. In this inner awareness, I release all outer, superficial concerns and I enjoy living.

27

I live in the joyous Light of God today and every day.

Even though I may not know what is ahead today, I say, "Thank You, God, for this day and the privilege of living it." I look forward to it.

Today, I enjoy everything that I do. I do that which God has given me to do. I express enthusiasm in my actions. I express love, kindness and interest in everyone around me.

I do good, today, even if it means going out of my way to do it. As I do a good turn, I store up a treasure in Heaven.

28

As I give, I know that I receive. The Spirit of generosity flows through me, today, making me whole on every level. Thank You, God, for this abundant life.

Infinite Joy wells up in me today. I am the channel of love through which all good things are expressed.

There is abundance everywhere. God has given me His great Kingdom. I am full of spiritual inspiration, of wisdom and ideas, and of love. My sound and wonderful body is the instrument through which I express joy.

Thank You, God, for the joy which is mine today. Thank You for the free, full flow of life surging through me. I think positively and creatively. I am always on Your side as You are always on my side. You are all of me. I am that part of You which I can understand.

29

The more I understand, the more I express joy in my world and the more I express God in all of my actions.

This is a beautiful day of joy and creative expression. I give thanks for Divine Inspiration. I give thanks for life and the privilege of expressing it. I give thanks for love and the joy of giving and receiving it.

I am inspired by the Infinite Presence within me and it is manifested in my success.

30

31 ***The Infinite Potential of my being is revealed to me and I am overjoyed.*** This is a day of success and achievement.

Today, I go forward into life to do that which God has given me to do. My thoughts are clear, my feelings are warm, my words are kind, my actions are controlled. I am in charge of myself. I am on top of things, and I consciously create good circumstances by thinking positively at all times. I am truly happy with my state of affairs.

Through the good will and cheerfulness that emanate from me, all things unfold in the best interest of myself and everyone concerned.

I am happy about things today. If sometimes I don't feel so, I turn my outlook around. I can always find something to be joyful about.

Monthly Goals

....
....
....
....
....
....
....
....
....
....
....
....
....
....
....
....
....
....
....

November

• P E A C E •

I EXPERIENCE PEACE IN ALL THINGS

I go to my inner center, and, as I live from this center, all things unfold in perfect order and peace in my world.

My thoughts are calm and ordered. I am attuned to the One Presence and the One Power.

My inner tranquility produces outer harmony in my world. Thank You, God, for the abundance of all good things. Thank You for the consciousness of peace, the consciousness of love and the consciousness of Light.

I am one with God and God is One with me. All good is taking place in my life. I give thanks that this is so.

Quietly, I attune myself to the inner flow of the Spirit. I find within myself Infinite Peace. I am surrounded in a protective Light and I feel a great sense of calm.

Today, I experience perfect peace—peace in my mind, peace in my heart, peace in my soul, peace in my body. God's Peace is established deeply within me. This peace is not found in the outer world, but comes from within me, from my walks upon the path of spiritual awakening.

1

There is peace on earth and it begins with me today. I am filled with peace and I share my peace with others.

I become still as I walk in the Light of the Spirit. I am filled with the consciousness of oneness and wholeness. I am filled with the peace that passeth all understanding.

2

Harmony and order flow out from me and temper the angry waves and rumblings of a harried, materialistic world. I help to bring about peace in my time by establishing peace in my own heart. I walk in peace today.

3 *I am poised and centered today, and nothing can disturb the serenity of my soul.* I experience calmness in all that I am and in all that I do.

I am the complete expression of God in action. I am attuned to all that is bright and beautiful. I feel the Divine Presence within me, blessing me with wholeness in every part of my life. I praise God from whom all blessings flow.

In awareness of God's calming Presence, I know that all is well.

4 *Today, our hearts beat as one.* We are free from all superficial concerns of any kind.

Peace is established in the hearts, minds and souls of all people. Peace is within the reach of all.

I find peace in my walks with God. His Presence is with me now and always.

Peace is established at the center of my being. I attune myself by first making myself calm and quiet. 5

Quietly and steadily, I travel to a higher level of spiritual awareness and understanding. I am thankful for God's guiding Presence on my spiritual path.

Today, I embrace quiet. Today, I reflect upon the nature of God, the nature of the universe, the nature of being. I may not be able to understand the great mystery of life, but I am calm. 6

Today, I take time to smell the flowers. Today, nothing can disturb the serenity of my soul. I am directed and inspired in all that I do.

7 *Quietly, I go inward to the dwelling place of the Infinite Kingdom.* I find there the Source of all love, all power, all beauty. These great gifts are a part of my life and my affairs.

I am blessed with an infinite abundance of gifts.

8 *I quiet my mind and go inward to the Secret Place of the Most High.*

Today, all of my selves—my physical self, my emotional self, my mental self, my spiritual self— are attuned to God.

I am a disciple. I follow God's direction on the path of spiritual growth. I endeavor to be an embodiment of His Love.

Today, I am free from fear, apprehension and concern. I am free from tension, pressure and confusion. God's Love casts out all of these.

9

I dwell in profound peace. I have faith that God is always present for me. I have faith in myself. I have faith in other people. I have faith in good prevailing.

The Kingdom of all good is within me. I do not need to search elsewhere.

10

When I turn inward and pray, I always find there the Source of Infinite Healing and Infinite Peace. I am nourished and have everything I need.

Today, I feel a deep inner peace. Harmony is unfolding in my life on every level and in every way.

11 **Pure, healing Light is shining down on me, filling me with a deep inner peace.** God is now present and active in my life and in all of my affairs. His Infinite Perfection is flowing into my soul, into my mind and into every cell in my body.

I am attuned and whole.

12 **I am attuned to the Infinite Oneness of the Spirit.** There is One Life and I live it joyously. There is One Truth and I know it clearly. There is One Love and I express it warmly.

God's great blessings bring me peace and assurance. I am a wonderful person, for I am made in His image and likeness. I have the Kingdom within me, for I consciously create circumstances of good for myself and others.

....

....

....

....

....

....

....

....

....

....

....

I feel the inspiring tide of Spirit in my life today. I am blessed with creative ideas and I allow their full expression in my world. **13**

I open myself up and Divine Energy flows into me making me whole. I experience peace of mind, soul and body. I experience success in all of my affairs. I experience harmony and peace in my relationships with other people.

....

....

....

....

....

....

....

....

....

....

....

Quietly, I contemplate the beauty and wonder which is within me. The Kingdom is my dwelling place. I live on the Wings of the Spirit and my consciousness soars to a higher level of awareness. **14**

I am filled with joyous enthusiasm for living and for helping others. I bless my fellow human beings and a great peace fills my being.

Harmony and Right Action are taking place in my life and in the lives of all people. I know there is a reason for everything and everything unfolds as it should.

15
I contemplate the Inner Reality, the Truth of my life.

God is all of me. I am that part of God which I can understand. I am His perfect child and I endeavor to live in such a way that His Wholeness may manifest Itself in every part of my being.

I am a peaceful being.

16
I bring all of my energies together and focus them on the goal of perfect awareness. I quiet all distracting thoughts and concerns.

As I attune my consciousness to a higher level of awareness, I feel good vibrating through every cell of my body. My body is a temple of the Living Spirit. I enjoy peace, strength and health.

I give thanks for this goodness in my life today.

Jack

....

This is my time to reside in the Shadow of the Almighty. 17

Thank You, God, for the peace that blesses my entire being. Thank You for the energy, the love and the creative power within me at all times. I am attuned to the perfect pattern of my perfect self known in the Mind of God.

I am complete. I am regenerated. I feel the process of rebirth taking place in me all of the time. I am perfectly balanced and peaceful now.

....

Nothing can come up, today, that God and I together cannot handle. 18 I am determined to overcome everything in the way of the realization of my potential. I am established in the consciousness of peace and harmony.

I am not afraid of anything. I go forward into life filled with the confidence and the faith that Right Action will prevail.

All good and peaceful blessings flow into my world and I share them with my loved ones. I live from the center of my oneness with God today.

19 *Peacefully, I contemplate the Infinite Presence, the complete and perfect Reality of being.*

Meditation is listening to God. Meditation is becoming centered in consciousness and tuning out all distracting thoughts and feelings. In meditation, I experience peaceful, silent, inner knowing.

I feel the workings of the Divine Presence in my life. I am grateful for the privilege of my sweet and joyous relationship with God.

20 *I am a peaceful person today, because I am in tune with the Infinite Healing Presence.* I am in tune with peaceful life.

God is the expression of peace in my being. I am a true expression of Him in every aspect of my life.

I treat others as God treats me—with love, consideration and attentiveness. I strive to be of service, today, to all I meet. Selfless, generous deeds to others are the surest road to God. I travel this pathway today and always.

I am dedicated to peace today. I am attuned to God and I feel the energy of His Love flowing into my being. Peace is settling over my whole being.

I dedicate myself, my life, my work—all that I am and all that I do—to the service of the Living One. I dedicate myself to spreading peace among my fellow human beings everywhere I go.

Thank You, God, for guiding our destiny. Thank You for healing, for comforting and for sustaining all of us in peacefulness.

21

Life has great purpose and meaning for all of us. We all have our place in the world, and, though our lives vary, we share the ultimate goal of self-realization. We all want to lead peaceful lives.

I receive the guidance I need from God to move in the right direction. I move forward to do mighty works, to be strong, to keep my chin up, my head high, my eyes bright, my face smiling and my step firm.

I do God's quiet work. God needs me and I need Him. Today, I express His Peace in all things.

22

23 *At this moment, I touch the Infinite Reality.* At this moment, I am one with all that is. The universal calm is flowing through me.

   The consciousness of peace is established in my mind, my heart, my soul and my body today.

   I express the perfection which is God. Infinite Abundance is taking place in every cell of my body right now. I am filled with the Reality of God in every part of my being.

24 *Today, I go forward into life filled with joy and peace.* Divine Order and Right Action are working in my life. I live from my inner center and nothing can disturb the serenity of my soul.

   I am at peace with myself and with the world.

Today, Infinite Reality is revealed to me. I am in contact with the fullness of life. I am one with all good flowing through me. I am a channel through which Infinite Abundance expresses itself. I am a channel through which Infinite Life flows.

Divine Peace is established in my mind, heart, soul and body. I am thankful for this gift from God.

25

As I reside at the center of my being, I feel God in action in my life.

Today, I assimilate the peace, the joy and the beauty of God into my life. I am in tune with the oneness of life. I feel the Divine Spirit moving through me, refreshing and uplifting me.

All problems are solved. All needs are met. There is nothing in my consciousness other than the state of tranquility.

26

27 *Quietly, I make contact with the Infinite Healing Presence.* Deeper and deeper into my inner awareness I go, deeper and deeper into the Infinite Peace. I experience a peace greater than any I have ever known.

Through my peaceful walks with God, I have increased intuition, awareness, inspiration and insight. These gifts are working for good in my life.

God, I give Thee thanks for the privilege of realizing my higher self.

28 *I dwell in the Divine Reality within and Infinite Peace fills my being.*

I take firm hold of my life, today, and I go on from this point. I live from the center of Light—Light that permeates my body, my mind and all of my world. I am grateful for this world of Light and Peace—a world fit to live in and a life worth living.

I am divinely protected today. I am in the midst of God's Love and Protection. The Infinite Healing Presence indwells every cell of my body, every aspect of my mind, every nuance of my thought and feeling. I am a perfect child of God.

The Living Light of the Spirit vibrates through me and sustains me in peace.

29

This is my time with God. This is my time to become still and know that the Kingdom is within me. This is my time to pray, to meditate, to be silent and listen.

Today, I have a profound sense of well-being. Nothing can disturb the serenity and harmony of my being. There is nothing I cannot do, no reason for worry, because God is with me now.

30

Monthly Goals

December

▪ SPIRITUAL UNDERSTANDING ▪

I AM IN CONTACT WITH SPIRIT

As I dwell, today, in the consciousness of God, I dedicate myself wholly to the awareness of Him. I dedicate my life to discipleship to Him. I dedicate myself to resurrecting God in my heart and in the hearts of all mankind.

My prayer inspires me toward greater realization of my true and perfect self. I am mentally clear, alert, attuned, and I am actively participating in my life. I am emotionally balanced. I am filled with love for all things in God's Universe.

I move forward, today, along the pathway of growth, unfoldment, spiritual understanding and self-realization. The Presence of God is personified and individualized in me, and I am whole in the consciousness of the One.

Thank You, God, for the faith that strengthens my heart and all of my endeavors. Thank You for spiritual understanding.

Spiritual understanding is the ability of the mind to comprehend and realize the Laws of God. It is the ability to let go of outer worldly concerns and focus on the inner world of self-knowing. Within each of us is the capacity to understand God and ourselves.

Understanding is knowing that power should be expressed through love, that zeal should be tempered with wisdom. Divine Understanding in us unites us with God. The Holy Spirit always knows what to do.

Today, I understand myself. I understand God and His Spiritual Laws.

1

I go deep within now to the heart of the subconsciousness. As I believe and feel in my heart, so am I.

I go into the subterranean area of my consciousness and release myself from imprisonment. I open the lid of the container and the great knowledge of the universe pours out.

All hostility is dissolved, all hatred is removed from my heart. My heart beats in rhythm with the Heart of the universe.

2

3 ***The abundant warmth of my heart is my true prosperity.*** My riches come from God. My heart is filled to overflowing with love and the conviction that God is my Supply.

God is the Cause of all things. All effects can be traced back to Him.

4 ***I absorb the richness and fullness of God in my life today.*** I am fulfilled in every way. I experience health, happiness, prosperity and love in all that I do no matter how insignificant. I embody all of the riches of the Kingdom in my actions. They flow out and become wonderful things in my world—wonderful things for me to share.

I am attuned to the Living Light of the Spirit shining down on me from above, illuminating Everlasting Life.

Quietly and gently, I touch the Divine Energy within and I experience the Reality of All-Lovingness. **5**

I live from the center of Light. Light permeates my body, my mind and all of my affairs. I am attuned to the Infinite Healing Presence that knows Itself in me and makes my life meaningful.

Thank You, God, for courage and faith to meet this day and every day. Thank You for the great adventure of life.

This day is a tremendous opportunity for me to go forth and do mighty works. **6**

My prosperity comes from an attitude that I create within and project onto the world. I am a positive and creative force.

I open the gates of my consciousness for the free fullness of life to flow through me. I am full of vitality and enthusiasm on my spiritual path of self-discovery. I am grateful that I have more than enough to meet all of my requirements and to accomplish all of my goals.

7 ***This is a beautiful day to discover the meaning and purpose of life.***

Today, I establish goals of my spiritual growth: to be more loving, to have stronger faith, to have a greater understanding of God. I set outer goals of achievement in my life: harmonious conditions, loving relationships, financial security, physical health.

I first set my inner goals, then my outer goals, and I move forward toward accomplishing them. I believe that I can accomplish anything that I set out to do.

8 ***Today is a time of silent, inner knowing.*** This is a day of attunement, of inner worship. Through this quiet time, I am gaining a world of spiritual prosperity.

I let the Source distribute Itself through my mind, heart, soul and body. I feel the Presence of God in my being. I am attuned to His Vitality.

Divine Understanding of the Holy Spirit gives me the insight to always know what to do. 9

I understand a great deal today. I understand the plan which God has in mind for me. I understand my part. When I pray, everything depends upon God, and when I work, everything depends upon me.

I understand that virtue is its own reward. I understand that there is a reason and meaning for all things and this gives me great security.

I am transformed by the renewal of my mind. 10

My mind is alive, alert and awake. My mind is perceptive and aware, filled with the vital understanding of how to relate and reason in my world.

My mind is clear. My mind is Light. I give thanks for my beautiful mind today. I give thanks for the perfection of God's Mind expanding in mine.

11 ***My mind is receptive and free from external conditioning.*** My mind is free from false belief. My mind is attuned to Truth. My mind is free from preconceptions and I am open to spiritual experience. My mind flows. I am grateful for a healthy mind with which to think, perceive and reach upward.

Thank You, God, for the Divine Energy that inspires and uplifts me.

12 ***I release all concern for outer things.*** I focus upon the serene inner awareness.

As I lie down in the green pastures of peacefulness, a great sense of well-being comes over me. I am made whole.

My mind, my heart, my soul—my entire identity with God—is strengthened through prayer. My work in this life is to build. As I build my life in the best way I can, other lives are touched and affected. We are all one in spiritual consciousness.

....

....

....

....

....

....

....

....

....

....

I obey the Law of the Spirit today.

13

I am free from limitation. I am free from lack. I move forward into abundant expression of good. I love freely.

Love is the tenet of my life. Grace is the result of my love. I walk with God. I affirm my oneness with Him.

I endeavor to be a perfect child of God. I move forward into a life of beautiful expression today.

....

....

....

....

....

....

....

....

....

....

I have a plan for my life. My plan is to perfect my spiritual understanding. My plan is to build a stately mansion of perfection in my soul. I have a strong desire to do this, to work with God in bringing this about.

14

The consciousness of the Spirit within me is strong and vital. I am filled with joy and enthusiasm on my spiritual pathway.

15 *I give thanks for this opportunity of introspection and affirmation.* Today, I learn the lessons of the soul. I am embarked upon the most beautiful journey of unfoldment.

I approach the lessons of the soul with a desire to change, a desire to grow, a desire to experience. I open myself to the peace, love, understanding and gentleness of God.

16 *I realize myself through prayer, meditation and good deeds.* The Grace of the Spirit is unfolding in my being.

I am filled with love and understanding, the great gifts of God. Love flows from my heart out to all people. It flows back to me from others, enriching my life.

As my understanding increases, I am more adjusted in my world. I am more aware of Divine Guidance showing the way on my journey.

This is a day of meditation and release. 17

When I pray, I let go of all distracting thoughts and focus on the Perfect One. I draw close to God in my prayer. I pray with Him. In my prayer, I am an expression of Him.

My prayer is my blending with God. As I draw near to Him, He draws near to me.

Through prayer, I am assured that all is well, that God is in His Heaven and all is right with the world.

It is my joy to live this day fully, to live every moment as though it were my first and my last. I 18 am filled with joy. I am filled with expectancy on my path towards spiritual awakening.

I give thanks for this day. I give thanks for the gift of life. I give thanks for the great mystery of the Spirit moving through me. I give thanks for the feeling deep down within me that there is more to life than there appears to be. There is always more to discover and experience.

19 *On this bright, beautiful day, I go forward with a mighty faith to do those things which God has given me to do.*

I realize greater power, greater potential, greater expression within. Divine Order and Right Action are unfolding in wonderful ways and I am achieving my goals.

The Light of God is a golden path that leads me to the summit of the mountain—the summit of great understanding.

20 *This is a bright, new day.* I fill my day with purposeful activity. Creative good flows into me, inspiring me to a higher level of awareness, and flows out from me reaching and helping people in all different ways.

This is my opportunity to live, to learn, to serve and to unfold into the expression of all good.

I give thanks for the work that I have to do. I give thanks for meaning and worth in my life.

Beauty is in the air. A sparkle is everywhere. I feel the abundance of God's Infinite Life surrounding and filling me with goodness. **21**

Today, I experience perfect health on every level. I experience the joy of living. I experience my spiritual unfoldment.

Thank You, God, for the resurrection that is taking place within me now.

As I walk in the consciousness of the Light, I become aware of the great scope of life. Smaller **22** concerns fall away.

I give thanks for this life and the privilege of living it. I give thanks for the world and the opportunity of experiencing it. I give thanks for other people and the privilege of growing closer together in the consciousness of God's Oneness.

I am so grateful for everything today. I take nothing for granted and fully enjoy everything.

23 *My heart beats in rhythm with the Heart of the universe.* I know that if I ask, I shall receive. If I seek, I shall find. If I knock, it cannot help but be opened unto me.

The abundance of life is surging through me on every level. I am mentally and emotionally balanced, and spiritually whole.

I am full of creative self-expression today. I know that there is something that I can do better than it has ever been done before.

24 *I am in tune with the healing forces within me.* I release all energy of anything unlike the Nature of God.

I am in tune with the perfect pattern of my perfect self. The channels are open. The Spirit is manifesting Itself in me. I am a whole, healthy, vital individual. I give thanks that this is so.

Today, I give thanks for Christmas, the ultimate expression of all wonderful things. I give thanks for the lessons of Christ which have opened my eyes, have expanded my consciousness. I learn again how to give and how to receive.

The message of Christmas circulates throughout the consciousness of all mankind at this blessed time. I can feel excitement in the air. There is more love and caring expressed everywhere and I am a part of it. I am part of the growing spiritual understanding.

25

This is a beautiful day for inner experience. This is a beautiful life to live.

As I explore the inner world, my consciousness is attuned to a higher vibration. My inner contact with the Spirit gives me a sense of purpose, a sense of meaning, a sense of continuity.

Everything I do, everything I touch is imbued with the larger significance of spiritual awareness. I am not the same person I was before I began on my spiritual path.

26

27 *This is a day of vibrant inner attunement to the Spirit.* This is a day of energy and accomplishment.

Today, I go forward into my life filled with vim and vigor. The full, flow of spiritual energy is circulating through my being. My body is strong, pure and capable. I climb the highest mountain in my quest for spiritual understanding.

28 *I behold the Spirit of God in everyone I see.* I am focused singly on the higher vibration and I see only good in my world. God is blessing everyone today and every day.

I behold the Perfection of God in my mind, my heart, my soul. I keep ever before me the image of my perfect self.

It is sometimes difficult to comprehend the scope of the great gifts that God has given to me, that I have all of His Blessings.

29

All that God has is mine—all of His Love, all of His Life, all of His great, beautiful Creation. I am a rich person indeed.

I ask God to guide me, today, to do that which is right for me.

My faith makes me whole. According to my faith, it is done unto me. Today, I am free from external concerns, worries, tensions or anxieties. I dwell in perfect peace because my mind is focused on the Spirit.

30

I become a channel through which God's Healing Light flows out and blesses myself and all others. I endeavor to help those less fortunate than myself.

31 **Today, I invoke Divine Guidance.** I know that God knows the way. I attune myself to God and He shows me the way.

I am thankful for spiritual understanding and for spiritual life. An entire new world has been revealed to me in my walks with God. I have learned a new way to live.

There is nothing I cannot do, no difficult situation I cannot handle. I have the greatest wisdom in the universe to help me overcome any obstacle. I can call on God any time I am in need.

Infinite Divine Inspiration is my teacher and I am guided on the path of righteousness all the days of my life.

Afterword

Now that you have completed a year of *Master Meditations,* you may want to note the many ways in which you, your work, your relationships, your faith have changed over the past year. In what ways are you stronger, wiser, more loving, more peaceful? Take a moment to contemplate how you have changed this past year through your increased awareness and concentrated focus on the good in your life. Your attitude of gratitude will continue to carry over into your life and the lives of all those you touch.

This is only the first year of your master meditations. Each year you use *Master Meditations,* you will increase your awareness, wisdom, joy, and understanding of yourself and your relationship to God.

Continue on your path. God bless you!

Name_____

Address_____

City_____State_____Zip_____

Book Title and Author	Quantity	Price	Total
Master Meditations: A Spiritual Daybook, *by Dr. Donald Curtis*		$12.95	
Axioms for Survivors: How to Live Until You Say Goodbye, *by Lon Nungesser*		6.95	
Good People: The Whole Self Integration Guide *by Ruth Cherry, Ph.D.*		12.95	
The Book of Rituals: Transformation Through Myth and Magic, *by Rev Carol Parrish-Harra*		14.95	
The Law of Mind in Action, *by Dr. Fenwicke Lindsay Holmes*		10.95	
The Laws of Wealth, *by Dr. Fenwicke Lindsay Holmes*		10.95	
When Your Parents Need You, *by Rita Robinson*		9.95	
Survivors of Suicide, *by Rita Robinson*		9.95	
The New Age Handbook on Death and Dying, *by Rev. Carol Parrish-Harra*		9.95	
Being Human in the Face of Death *by Deborah Roth, MSC & Emily LeVier, MSC*		9.95	
Stepping Stones to Grief Recovery, *by Deborah Roth, MSC*		8.95	
Gifts for the Living: Conversations with Caregivers on Death & Dying, *by BettyClare Moffatt, M.A.*		9.95	
	Sales Tax 6.5% (California Only)		
	Shipping/Handling ($2.00 per book)		
	Total Due		

Please send check or money order to:

IBS PRESS, Inc.
744 Pier Avenue
Santa Monica, CA 90405
(213)450-6485

O R D E R   F O R M

FOLD ALONG DOTTED LINE

IBS PRESS, INC.
744 PIER AVENUE
SANTA MONICA, CA 90405

PLACE
STAMP
HERE